Books by Albert Marrin

The Airman's War
Overlord
Victory in the Pacific
The Sea Rovers
War Clouds in the West
1812: The War Nobody Won
The Secret Armies
Aztecs and Spaniards
The Yanks Are Coming
Struggle for a Continent

Struggle for a Continent

STRUGGLE FOR

A CONTINENT:

THE FRENCH

AND INDIAN WARS

➤➤➤ 1690-1760 ◄◄◄

91-15267

by Albert Marrin

New York · ATHENEUM · *1987*

Atheneum
Macmillan Publishing Company
866 Third Avenue, New York, NY 10022
Collier Macmillan Canada, Inc.

Composition by Haddon Craftsmen, Allentown, Pennsylvania
Printed and bound by Fairfield Graphics, Fairfield, Pennsylvania
Map drawn by Bruce Hiscock
Designed by Mary Ahern
First Edition

10   9   8   7   6   5   4   3   2   1

Library of Congress Cataloging-in-Publication Data

Marrin, Albert.
Struggle for a continent.

Bibliography: p. 213
Includes index.
1. United States–History–King William's War, 1689–1697
Juvenile literature.   2. United States–History–Queen Anne's War,
1702–1713–Juvenile literature.
3. United States–History–King George's War, 1744–1748–Juvenile
literature.   4. United States–History–French and Indian War,
1755–1763–Juvenile literature.   I. Title.
E196.M4   1987   973.2   86-26508
ISBN 0-689-31313-6

For my parents,
Louis and Frieda Marrin

Contents

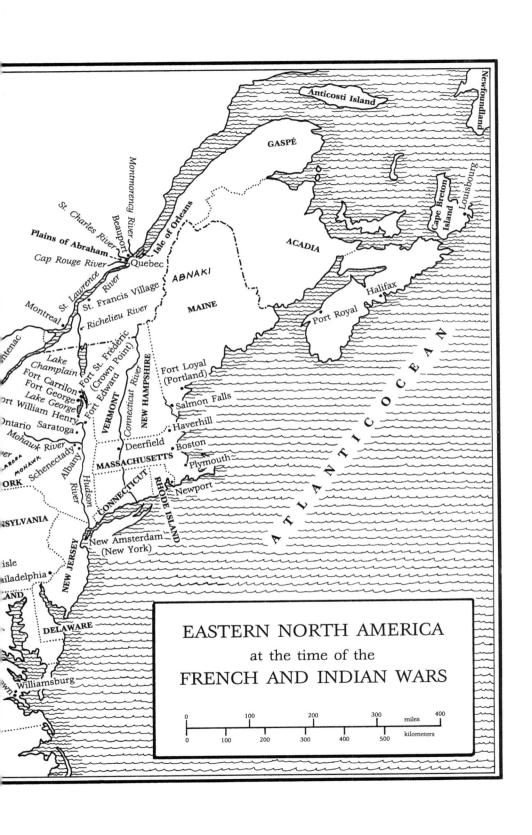

EASTERN NORTH AMERICA

at the time of the

FRENCH AND INDIAN WARS

. . . notwithstanding the treachery of their neighbors the French, and the cruelty of their neighbors the Indians . . . this will, some time hence, be a vast empire, the seat of power and learning. Nature has refused them nothing, and there will grow a people out of our little spot, England, that will fill this vast space.

—James Wolfe writing to his mother, August 11, 1758,
describing America and the Americans

Struggle for
a Continent

Prologue:
Blood on the Snow

FEBRUARY 8, 1690: a bitterly cold night with wind gusts blowing white spray from the tops of giant snowdrifts. Ice-clad branches sway, ghostlike, in the breeze. Overhead, the stars of the Milky Way splash, bright and distant, across the cloudless sky.

Schenectady, a settlement of fifty families on the Mohawk River in New York colony, lay under a mantle of fresh snow. There had been a celebration earlier in the evening, and the rum had flowed freely. For a few hours, the villagers—simple, industrious folk—could forget the hardships of frontier living. Now they slept soundly, safe and snug beneath heaps of blankets. All was still, save for the crackling of dying embers in the fireplaces.

It was so peaceful that even the tiny militia unit was asleep in the blockhouse. The gate of the log wall surrounding the village stood wide open, blocked by a snowdrift. Only two snowmen with broomstick-muskets kept watch on either side of the gate, their charcoal eyes staring blankly at the tree line across the clearing.

At midnight, figures swaddled in buckskin and fur emerged from the woods. They moved swiftly, the scraping of their snowshoes lost in the wailing of the wind. Each cradled a musket in his arms; thrust into his belt was a knife with a long, tapering blade and a wicked-looking hatchet. Nearly half the men had mustaches and bushy beards flecked with ice where their breath had frozen on contact. Their companions, however, had no facial hair. Instead, their faces were painted with bright circles and triangles, lines, and zigzags. Most had colored stones dangling from their earlobes; several wore silver rings thrust through their nostrils.

Obeying their officers' hand signals, two hundred French Canadians and Indians slipped past the snowmen and through the gate. When every house was surrounded, a war whoop burst from the Indians' throats. The sound pierced the cabins' log walls, echoing in the sleepers' ears. But it was already too late.

The raiders sprang forward, smashing doors open, tearing window shutters from hinges, and screaming. Always screaming. Settlers died in their beds—shot, stabbed, and clubbed by unseen assassins. By daybreak, sixty people, including infants, were dead. Except for the few who escaped in the confusion, all the others were taken prisoner and Schenectady burned. The captives, terrified and whimpering, hands bound with leather thongs, were herded northward toward Canada. Behind them nothing remained but ashes, bodies, and bloody snow.

Nobody could have known it then, but this night of terror was the first in a conflict that would rage on and off for seventy years. Although each of the four stages of this conflict had its own name—King William's War, Queen Anne's War, King George's War, the French and Indian War—they were really part of a single, gigantic struggle called the French and Indian Wars. It was the most savage, the most cruel war ever waged in North America. For it was nothing less than a struggle for a continent of breathtaking beauty and boundless riches. And whoever controlled that continent might well become the most powerful nation on earth.

⇛ I ⇚

Three Peoples

THREE VERY DIFFERENT PEOPLES took part in the struggle for North America: Indians, French, English, each strong and proud of its heritage. Each thought its own ways best, the others' inferior or, what is worse, evil. To understand their struggle, we must first understand their ways of life.

The ancestors of the American Indians were the first humans to set eyes on the New World. Some time between twenty-five thousand and thirty thousand years ago, during the last Ice Age, immense glaciers covering thousands of square miles slid down from the North Pole. Eventually these slow-moving rivers of ice covered much of the Northern Hemisphere, leveling hills and gouging out valleys.

With so much of the earth's water trapped in the form of ice, some of the higher areas of the ocean bottoms rose above the waves. One of these areas formed a land bridge several hundred miles wide spanning the Bering Strait between Siberia and Alaska. Slowly, during many centuries, bands of Asiatic hunters crossed the land bridge in search of game.

The world they entered, though uninhabited by humans, was anything but empty. At the fringes of the glaciers and beyond lay dense forests, rolling grasslands, and rugged mountain ranges. The land teemed with strange creatures. Prehistoric America echoed with the hoofbeats of vast herds of bison, twice as large as any today, and wooly mammoths, giant elephants with tusks fifteen feet long. Saber-toothed tigers stalked their prey around water holes or ran it down in the open.

The hunters moved southward, always southward, following the herds. In time, the prehistoric animals died out, their places taken by creatures familiar to us. As the earth warmed, the glaciers halted and then, melting, retreated. The Bering Strait land bridge vanished beneath the Pacific Ocean once more, stranding the hunters. Like it or not, they became Americans with a vast new world to explore.

Thousands of years passed, during which these first Americans advanced from Alaska to the tip of South America. The Eskimo, the last group to migrate from Siberia, remained in the far north, content to live in icehouses and hunt the whale, seal, walrus, and polar bear. Aztecs and Mayas built sprawling temple-cities in the highlands and jungles of Mexico and Central America. Apache and Navajo learned to live in the scorching deserts of the Southwest. Sioux, Cheyenne, and Comanche discovered the Great Plains, that land of big sky and swaying grass between the Mississippi River and Rocky Mountains.

Perhaps six thousand years ago, several peoples arrived in the Eastern Woodland Wilderness. A sea of green stretched unbroken from behind the sand dunes of the Atlantic shore to the Mississippi, from the swamps of Georgia and Florida to the pine forests of Canada. Here trees—pine, oak, hickory, maple, walnut, birch, and poplar—grew in uncounted millions. Except for the needly pine, these trees have wide, green leaves that turn fiery red and orange and brown before dropping off in the fall. They grew so tall and thick that the sun barely filtered through their interlocking branches. Anyone walking among them from April to October moved in a shimmering green haze.

The Eastern Woodland Wilderness is gone now, destroyed by the ax to make way for the plow. All that remains is the memory of it preserved in Indian legend and the writings of white travelers who saw it in its glory.

About three hundred thousand Eastern Woodland Indians inhabited this wilderness when Columbus first set sail. It fed them, clothed them, sheltered them, and gave them protection. By far, the largest number of these Indians belonged to the Algonquian family. "Algonquian" is not the name of a tribe*, but of a family of languages. Algonquian-speaking peoples inhabited the entire northeastern quarter of today's United States and much of southern Canada. The coastal Algonquian—the Pequot, Massachuset, Narraganset, Powhatan—welcomed the early English settlers and taught them to survive in a strange land; we remember that help every year at Thanksgiving. By the 1690s, however, the newcomers had broken the power of the coastal tribes and had taken their best lands.

Yet their inland cousins still controlled a vast domain around the Great Lakes and the lands drained by the Mississippi and Ohio river systems. Illinois, Kickapoo, Menomini, Miami, Chippewa, Ottawa, Potawatomi, Sauk and Fox: Each tribe claimed lands that seemed to have belonged to it since the beginning of time.

Whatever their tribe, the inland Algonquian shared a similar way of life. They lived in villages of about two hundred people, built on a narrow strip of land jutting into a lake or river and protected by a log wall. Algonquian favored two types of homes. The *wigwam* was made of slender poles driven into the ground and bent to form a dome. The *tepee* was cone shaped, with poles

---

*The Algonkian, however, were a tribe of Algonquian-speaking Indians who lived along the St. Lawrence River in Canada.

set up at angles and tied where they crisscrossed at the top. Unlike the Plains tribes, who covered their tepees with buffalo hide, forest dwellers used the white and silvery gray bark of the birch tree.

Birchbark was prized for its many uses. Lightweight, tough, and plentiful, it contains an oil that makes it waterproof. It can be folded and sewn with vines to make containers and cooking pots; water was boiled simply by dropping in heated stones. Birchbark canoes carried heavy loads, handled easily, and could be repaired with a glue made from tree sap. Campers still use strips of birchbark to kindle fires in damp wood.

The birchbark-covered home, waterproof and cozy, had space for a family, its possessions, and its pet dogs. Still, it was a tight fit, and nobody dreamed of privacy. The idea that people should have their own rooms and sleep by themselves would have seemed strange, even funny, to the Algonquian. Everyone—husband, wife, children, visitors, in-laws, dogs—slept close to each other around the low fire that was kept burning always. And, summer or winter, they slept naked. It make a lot of sense to sleep this way. Birchbark crawled with bugs, as did buckskin clothing, and it was best not to give these tiny terrors comfortable nesting places. Thus, in summer everyone slept on the ground on mats woven by the women. In winter they slept together under furs, sharing their body warmth. Indian youngsters learned the facts of life early.

Families also bathed together, often inviting friends and neighbors to join them. Each village had its sweat lodge—a low, windowless shed of wood and mud built beside a stream. Men, women, and children sat around a pile of heated rocks, pouring water over it from time to time. Indians, who had no soap, relied upon sweating to clean their bodies and cure certain sicknesses. When the sweat lodge filled with steam, and the heat became unbearable, they dived naked into the stream or, in winter, rolled in the snow.

An Indian village three centuries ago was more peaceful than any European city of the time or an American city today. There were no muggings, no riots, no professional criminals.

Each village had its chief and council of elders—men (but not women) respected for their wisdom. Everything concerning the community was discussed and decided by the wise men before taking action. Yet this wasn't a real government with police and courts and tax collectors. These didn't exist among the woodland tribes. Chief and council led by example and persuasion, often through very long, poetic speeches; Indians loved oratory and could spend whole days listening to speeches. If the people weren't persuaded, however, nothing could make them obey.

Indian villages had little crime because they allowed many things white people considered wrong. Since religion was a private affair with them, nobody suffered for their beliefs. Fighting was no crime, nor, for that matter, were stealing and murder. Whenever someone was wronged, he or she looked to themselves and their families for justice, not to the tribe. A victim was allowed, if he could, not only to take back his property by force, but to take the thief's property as well.

Punishing murder was the duty of the victim's family. Killing a person triggered a "blood feud" in which any of the victim's relatives could kill any of the murderer's relatives in revenge. Revenge had to be taken; otherwise, the victim's ghost could never rest in peace. To stop a blood feud, which might claim scores of lives over the years, the murderer's family gave valuable presents to the victim's family in payment for his life. Europeans called this payment "blood money."

Witchcraft—using magic to harm others—was the only crime punished by the community. When the council decided that someone was a witch, a warrior was appointed to crush his or her head with a club when least expected. Indians knew nothing of trial by jury, police, or prisons.

Wilderness living was difficult and dangerous, so that every life was precious; a tribe could never have too many people. A birth was good news, celebrated with feasting, dancing, and gift giving. After all, children were the tribe's future, the guarantee of its existence through the ages.

Indians were gentle, kindly parents who openly showed love for their children. An infant, or *papoose* in Algonquian, was swaddled in beaver skins and tied to a cradle board, a straight wooden plank that kept it from moving. This allowed its bones to grow straight and strong by the time it was ready to walk. Mother could easily carry the cradle board strapped to her back, stand it nearby while at work, or hang it on a tree out of earshot if the papoose's crying became a nuisance.

When a child began to toddle, mother gave it as much freedom as possible. For she knew that wherever it roamed in the village there would be adults and older children to keep it from harm. Any child could invite itself into any wigwam and be sure of finding kind words, a soft pat, and a warm hug.

Children learned early that they were free people, that an Indian never ordered a family member or a fellow tribesman to do anything. But freedom didn't mean freedom to do wrong. Indians had a strong moral code. Parents constantly lectured youngsters about their duties. A good person, they insisted, was truthful, honest, and respectful of others. People must be generous, sharing with those less fortunate than themselves. As long as there was food in the village, nobody need go hungry. The poorest person had only to walk into a wigwam and sit by the fire to be served without a word being spoken. Being fed was not cause for giving thanks, but a basic human right, like breathing the air.

Parents never raised their voices, let alone their hands, when children misbehaved. All Indians thought shouting, except in games and war, undignified, a sign of poor upbringing. Hitting or slapping in the face was an insult that called for bloody vengeance.

Naughty youngsters were quietly taken aside and reasoned

with until they saw their error. Failing this, they were shamed before relatives and friends. To be embarrassed and laughed at were the worst punishments a proud person could suffer.

Indian youngsters had no doubts about who they were or how they would make their way in the world. They had no choices and, hence, no doubts. The tribe expected girls to become women, boys men, each living up to his or her special responsibilities.

School was the home, the village, and the woodlands themselves. Girls followed their mothers about in order to learn "womanly" things firsthand. There was plenty to learn. A *squaw,* Algonquian for "woman," tended a small vegetable garden, growing corn, beans, and squash. She cooked the family's food, preserved meat by smoking it over a fire, and gathered firewood. The only time she didn't have to collect firewood was on her wedding day, when the other squaws brought it to her by the armload.

A squaw made her family's clothing from animal skins she'd tanned with a mixture of bark and deer brains; she softened the new leather by chewing it, which usually caused her to lose her teeth by the age of thirty. Sewing was done not by pulling thread with a needle, but with a bone awl. A hole was made in a piece of leather with an awl; then a length of sinew-thread made of thin strips of deer muscle was passed through it and knotted into place. Buckskin garments lasted for years, although moccasins wore out quickly, so that new pairs were always being made. Squaws decorated their handiwork with dyed porcupine quills arranged in striking patterns.

A boy became a man by proving himself as a hunter. Although the Algonquian grew some food, meat was the basis of their diet. The Eastern Woodland Wilderness held some of the finest game animals in the world. Fish, turtles, beaver, ducks, and geese swarmed in its waterways. Birds roosted in its treetops or, like the wild turkey, waddled through the underbrush. Animals large and small—bear, deer, moose, woodchuck, rabbit, mink, marten—roamed freely. These creatures were abundant and made good eating *if* you knew how to catch them.

The Algonquian knew. As soon as a boy-child could walk, his father gave him a miniature set of bow and arrows. Patiently, lovingly, his father taught him to bend the bow, aim, and shoot. As the boy-child grew, so did the bow, until he could bring down a deer at fifty yards.

The boy learned to "read" the woods like an open book. Father and son would lie hidden in the brush for hours—looking, listening, and studying nature's ways together. Everything that happened had meaning, which hunters had to understand and use to their advantage. Bent blades of grass told what animals, or people, had passed, and when, and how many. Long scratches on a tree trunk meant that a bear had its winter den nearby. Deer bounding through the forest by day or an owl's off-key screeching at night were warnings as sharp as any alarm bell.

By the time an Algonquian boy was twelve, he knew how to handle any situation in the woods. He marked out hunting areas and told companions where he'd gone with blazes notched in trees. He made a deadfall of logs and stones to break a bear's neck when it went for the bait he had set out, or he snared grouse with a noose attached to a bent sapling. Making a fire was easy for him, a matter of rubbing two sticks together or rotating a stick between his palms against a block of dry wood.

Hunting was more than killing one's next meal; it was a deeply religious experience. All American Indians believed that animals, like humans, had spirits or souls that were separate from their bodies. Animal spirits lived in secret villages, each with its own chief. Moose spirits had their villages, fox spirits theirs, and so on through the animal kingdom.

Animal spirits enjoyed taking physical form and roaming the earth, where the Indians hunted them. Killing them was all right, for although the animal died, the Indians believed its spirit returned to its village, from where it watched how the hunters treated its former body. Spirits were very sensitive, and if their bodies weren't treated properly, they would refuse to take physical form again, bringing starvation to the Indians.

According to Indian belief, all life is sacred, a gift from the Master of Life. When they hunted, it was because they needed food, not for entertainment. They killed regretfully, prayerfully, and with respect. Before the bear hunt, a Chippewa medicine man or priest beat his drum and sang to the bear-spirit: "O my brother! We are very hungry; we are on the point of starving and wish you to have pity on us, and tomorrow when the young men go out to hunt you, I want you to show yourself. I know very well that you are concealed somewhere close to my camp here. . . . I wish you would have pity on us and give us your body so that we may eat and not starve."

As they killed the bear, the hunters chanted their apologies. To make sure that there were no hard feelings, a tobacco pipe was placed in the dead bear's mouth and smoke blown down its throat in gratitude to its spirit. The Indians considered tobacco sacred, and its smoke gladdened the Master of Life. Even plants received apologies before the harvest and the fields were sprinkled with powdered tobacco afterward.

Wasting food was sinful and sure to anger the animal spirits. Everything was eaten, including the fat, intestines, and eyes. Any bones not used in toolmaking were handled with care. Bones of water creatures were returned to the water. Bones of land animals were given a decent burial or hung high in a tree with a prayer, out of reach of the village dogs.

The Algonquian, like other Indians, showed "two faces": one to outsiders, the other among themselves. Outsiders—other Indians and whites—knew them as solemn, stony-faced people of few words. But at home, among those they trusted, it was another matter. Villages were bustling, happy places, especially after the hunters returned with the winter meat supply. Now people took time out for festivals, to listen to storytellers, and to play games.

A favorite game of the woodland tribes was snow snakes, played with a long, flexible stick that slid along the frozen ground with the wavelike motion of a snake. During winter, a log, or a boy, was dragged through the snow to form a trough about a thousand feet long and ten inches deep; its sides and bottom were then packed down to make a smooth, icy surface. The game's object was to slide a "snake" down the trough, making it travel as far as possible, while opponents on the sidelines shouted and waved as a distraction.

In the moccasin game, you had to guess under which of four moccasins a pebble was hidden.

Indians were reckless gamblers who'd bet everything—clothes, canoes, weapons, tepees—on a single play. Once, in mid-winter, a group of men returned from a gambling visit to friends in another village. They walked barefoot through three feet of snow, laughing all the way.

THE ALGONQUIAN TRIBES shared the woodlands with the *Irinakhoiw* (real rattlesnakes), pronounced "Iroquois" by the first French explorers. Like the Algonquian, the Iroquois weren't a separate tribe, but peoples speaking any of the Iroquoian family of languages. The Erie and Huron, for whom two of the Great Lakes are named, were Iroquoian-speakers, as were the Cherokee of the South.

The most famous Iroquois called themselves "the People of the Longhouse." The English knew them as the Five Nations, since their confederacy, or alliance, was made up at first of five tribes.

In colonial times, the Five Nations controlled a wide band of territory in northern New York. From east to west, from the Hudson River to Lake Erie, they were the Mohawk, Oneida, Onondaga, Cayuga, and Seneca tribes. Later on, in 1713, the Tuscarora joined their cousins as the sixth nation, although the alli-

A warrior of the Five Nations at rest, posing with a long tomahawk pipe, in J. Grasset de St. Sauveur's Costumes Americaines *(1787).*

ance remained known as the Five Nations. A southern tribe, the Tuscarora had been driven from their homes by land-hungry Englishmen.

The Five Nations lived in villages of between two and three hundred people, protected by walls of logs stood upright in the ground. Their homes, the famous longhouses, were just that—long houses. Families shared one-story buildings as much as 240 feet long by 40 feet wide, built of a framework of beams covered by layers of elm bark. A central aisle with fires placed every few yards stretched from end to end, each fire serving two families. The building had no windows, and the fires were used for light as well as heat and cooking. On either side of the aisle were pairs of open shelves one above the other. This was home.

Each family ate and slept, lived and died, on a shelf thirteen feet long by six feet wide. The lower, or living, shelf was without curtain or screen, offering no privacy whatsoever. The upper shelf was the same size and used to store the family's possessions: tools, weapons, canoe paddles, cradle boards, furs, snowshoes, clay pots, clothing. Hanging from the longhouse's rafters were strings of drying apples, bundles of tobacco leaves, ears of corn, and anything else that needed a place.

Longhouses weren't for the weak or sensitive. The only fresh air came from tiny smoke holes in the roof, and these were shut in bad weather. Hot, stuffy, and crowded, longhouses were usually filled with eye-stinging smoke. The smoke often became so thick that people had to lie on the floor to avoid suffocation. Worse, the place stank, and there was nothing you could do to escape the foul odor, a blend of sweat and tobacco, ripening corn and babies, rancid fat and boiled meat. Fleas and wood lice kept everyone scratching and slapping. Dogs were constantly underfoot, running, yelping, and dirtying the earthen floor.

Longhouses, unlike modern apartment houses, weren't open to anyone who could pay the rent. Each longhouse was reserved for members of a clan, a large family grouping having common ancestors. Clans took their names not from people, but from animals whose spirits were believed to protect them, such as the Turtle, Bear, Wolf, Beaver, Deer, Hawk, Snipe, and Heron. Men usually had their clan emblem tattooed on their bodies; it was always painted on a board over the longhouse door.

The oldest woman, called "mother," was the most important person in any longhouse. No women anywhere in the world had more power than those of the Five Nations. Men owned their clothing and weapons. Everything else belonged to the longhouse mother and her female relatives: daughters, granddaughters, sisters, cousins, and nieces. The longhouses were theirs. Women, who did all the farming, owned the fields and the crops grown in them. This arrangement made sense. Since the younger, more active men were away for weeks at a time, hunting or following the warpath, the women had to keep things running smoothly at home.

Mothers decided whom their children would marry and when. One rule was always followed in choosing mates: Youngsters must marry outside their own clan. A girl of the Seneca Deer, for example, could marry a boy of any of the Five Nations' other clans, but never another Deer. Young girls were usually given to older men who could take care of them, boys to widows who were good workers. Husbands had to move into their wives' longhouses, where they treated their mothers-in-law with the greatest respect.

Children belonged to their mother's clan; their father's people had no rights over them and were, in effect, strangers. A Seneca Deer was treated as family by all the Deer in his or her own village. He or she was also welcome in any Deer longhouse of the Five Nations. If a marriage broke up, it was the husband who went away, leaving the children with their mother. Yet they were never without a fatherly man nearby. Their mother's brothers called them "son" and "daughter," and they knew them as "father." Her brothers deserved the name, for they took over all of the absent father's responsibilities.

The longhouse mothers also chose the tribal chiefs and the high chiefs, or *sachems,* who formed the Council of the Five Nations. This was real power, for although chiefs and sachems had to be men, they were accountable to women. Women decided what issues the council would discuss; sometimes they told the sachems exactly what to say. If a chief or sachem displeased the longhouse mothers, they'd warn him three times. If he didn't improve, they "removed his horns"—took away the antlers he wore as a sign of office.

The Council of the Five Nations began about the year 1500. At that time, there were no Five Nations, only five separate tribes filled with hatred for one another. Tribes fought over hunting grounds, for glory, and to avenge those killed in past wars. If they had gone on this way much longer, they would have ended by destroying themselves. The Algonquian tribes, who hated them, would have then controlled the entire northeastern wilderness.

Just when things seemed darkest, two men found the answer to the problem of survival. The first was Dekanawidah *(Dee-Kan-a-Wee-Da)*, a mysterious holy man from the land of the Huron. We know nothing about Dekanawidah, except that his name means "He, the Thinker."

One night Dekanawidah had a dream that would change the Indians' world. He saw a giant spruce tree reaching into the clouds and anchored to the ground by five roots. The roots grew, not in normal earth, but in soil made up of justice, sanity, goodwill, health, and peace. The dream, he believed, was the Master of Life's way of telling the Five Nations to end their quarrels and live as brothers.

Dekanawidah repeated his dream in village after village, but found few listeners. Although very handsome, he stuttered and could hardly make himself understood.

He was beginning to despair when he met a Mohawk chief named Hiawatha *(Hee-a-Wa-Tha)* who believed the dream. Hiawatha became the tongue of He, the Thinker, carrying his message among the longhouses. In time, he persuaded the tribes to set up the League of the Great Peace. Each member remained independent, governing itself without league interference. Once a year, the Five Nations sent representatives, the sachems, to a sort of congress in the Onondaga country. There, seated around the council fire, they discussed matters of common concern: trade, dealings with outsiders, war.

As the women looked on, each sachem spoke in turn, repeating the others' arguments and explaining why he agreed or disagreed with them. In this way, he showed that he understood the issue and would vote intelligently. Votes had to be unanimous. If even one sachem disagreed, the council would continue discussion and voting until either he or the others changed their minds. Thus, whatever the Five Nations decided to do, they did together as friends and allies.

But whatever happened, the Five Nations swore never again to fight among themselves. If tribes quarreled, they asked the council to work out a solution both could accept. No wonder Benjamin Franklin and other Founding Fathers of our country admired the Five Nations' system of government and had it in mind when the time came to draft the Constitution of the United States.

THE LEAGUE OF THE GREAT PEACE made the Five Nations strong, but it didn't bring peace to the woodlands. Nothing short of a miracle could have done that.

The woodland tribes went to war regularly and often. A year seldom passed without some raiding and killing, for war, to the Indian, was normal, as much a part of the world as sunrise and sunset. There had always been war and, as far as he knew, always would be.

To be a man was to be a warrior. A boy knew that in training to be a hunter he was also preparing for the warpath. He learned that a man must not only have courage, but be able to endure pain without flinching or crying out.

Everything possible was done to toughen him and build stamina. Groups of friends were sent on marathons, racing through the forest mile after mile, hour after hour. Small boys rubbed their foreheads together until pain forced one of them to give up. Teenagers tested their courage by bashing themselves against boulders until the blood came. Bruises and scars were like medals—signs that they were becoming men.

Woodlanders always had something to fight about. A distant tribe ambushed a hunting party trespassing on its lands. Or a man died in a brawl while visiting another village. In either case, braves had to take the warpath in revenge. Other wars came about because women demanded them. Any woman could call for vengeance if any of her menfolk were killed by outsiders. If a relative died of natural causes, she might ask that a captive be given to the family to take their place. That captive could only be taken in battle or by raiding an enemy village.

The decision to go to war, even by the Council of the Five Nations, didn't mean that tribes called out their armies. There were no Indian armies, for even the largest tribes had only a few hundred warriors. The Five Nations' fifteen hundred braves were the most of any woodland people's, although these averaged only three hundred per tribe.

Nor were there any Indian generals. A general makes plans and gives orders, which his troops must obey or face punishment. Tribal war leaders, however, did nothing of the kind. Anyone who wanted to lead a war party could do so, anytime, if he could get braves to follow him. Anyone who wanted to fight was welcome to join in, but nobody could make a brave fight.

Dressed to kill. A warrior, armed to the teeth, brandishes an enemy scalp drying at the end of his musket. Note the snowshoes on his feet. From Costumes Americaines.

A brave joined a war party because he trusted the leader, a warrior of experience and luck. Yet the leader had no authority over his followers. All he could do was give advice and lead by example, which the braves might ignore for any reason. If you disagreed with his plan or felt unlucky that day, you simply left the war party and went home. No one asked why you returned without the others; that wasn't anyone's business but your own.

Whenever someone decided to lead a raid, he went up to the village war post, a beam set firmly in the ground. He shouted his war cry and began the war dance. Then, with all his might, he struck the war post with a hatchet painted red and decorated with red feathers. As others joined the dance, he slowly led them through the village, picking up more braves as they went.

A leader might also send a war belt of wampum to invite braves from friendly tribes to join his party. The woodland Indians, having no written language, communicated by means of tiny colored beads arranged in patterns on belts—*wampum.* The beads were made by cutting clam shells into strips, boring holes in them with stone drills, and stringing them in long strands sewn together to form belts. Clam shells were brought from the coast by Indian traders who passed from tribe to tribe.

Wampum came in thousands of patterns and color combinations, each with its special meaning. White wampum announced that travelers came in peace, or that one side wanted to end a war. Red wampum with the figure of a hatchet woven in the corner, or black wampum wrapped around the actual weapon, were an invitation to join in a war.

Before taking the warpath, each brave made sure that he looked the part. Looking right not only told others that he was courageous, but might actually save his life.

White travelers in colonial times seldom, if ever, reported seeing Indians with mustaches or beards. Indians naturally have little body and facial hair, and any they had was thought ugly. Men spent hours carefully—painfully—plucking hair from their faces, chests, and underarms with mussel-shell tweezers. The hair on either side of their heads was also plucked, leaving a narrow crest or scalp lock, which made it difficult for an enemy to grab their hair during close combat. Unlike the tribes of the Great Plains, whose braves wore gorgeous war bonnets in which each feather represented an heroic act, the woodlanders used few feathers, and then only for decoration. One or two colorful feathers stuck in his scalp lock was enough for any brave.

Paint was another matter. A brave would sooner leave his weapons behind than go without war paint. The woodlanders constantly painted themselves with clays and vegetable colors mixed with bear grease. Squaws colored the parts in their hair, cheeks, eyelids, and ear rims with scarlet bloodroot. Children wore paint before clothes. Warriors streaked their faces and bodies with red, yellow, and white paint.

Paint had many uses. In summer, it was an excellent suntan lotion and insect repellent. Painted dancers pleased the animal spirits during festivals in their honor. Each warrior had his own design, given him by a spirit in a dream. Designs weren't meant to be ugly or to frighten the enemy. Bold and exciting, war designs were magical armor to protect the brave and strengthen his courage. Belief in their designs was often so strong that it gave warriors the extra willpower needed to fight their way out of dangerous situations.

Indian weapons were light but deadly at close range. Each brave made his own weapons, as his father had taught him, or traded for them from aged warriors who worked at the craft full-time. Since the woodlanders had no iron until the whites arrived, their weapons were of stone, bone, and wood. Knives, arrowheads, and spearpoints were made of razor-sharp pieces of flint. The *tomahawk*, Algonquian for "cutting tool," was a stone-headed hatchet; although it became dull quickly, it could easily knock chunks of wood out of a tree or be thrown at an enemy's head.

The brave's most fearsome weapon was the war club. Carved from a single piece of hardwood, the war club was two feet long and had a five-inch ball at the end. The ball sometimes resembled a head or face; often a piece of bone or stone was wedged into it for good measure. Another war-club design replaced the ball with a deer-horn spike set into the lower edge. Both types could crack a skull, break an arm, or cave in a rib cage in an instant. The light wooden shield braves carried might stop an arrow but was useless against the war club's crushing blows.

War parties traveled lightly. In addition to his weapons, each member carried an extra pair of moccasins and battle rations—a bearskin bag of corn flour and maple sugar attached to his belt. This high-energy food was nutritious and didn't need a cooking fire, which might alert the enemy to a war party in its territory. A brave could keep going all day on a handful of corn flour swallowed with water.

The warpath was exactly that—a path in the forest used by warriors to invade enemy territory unobserved. The main warpath of the Five Nations ran from the Hudson River to Lake Erie. It was about a foot wide and worn six inches deep from constant use. Many ancient warpaths have since become paved highways.

Swiftly, without saying a word or snapping a twig, the braves walked the warpath "Indian file," one behind the other. Woodlanders, unlike plainsmen, never used horses in war. The horse, a native of the Old World, was brought to the Americas by the Spanish explorers. The Great Plains, with their open spaces and tall grass, were ideal horse country; the Sioux and their cousins became fine cavalrymen. The woodlanders, however, never took to the horse, nor the horse to them. There is no room for horses to charge in dense forests; nor is there grass, except in clearings, for them to eat; horses won't feed on leaves or the bark of trees. The woodlanders valued captured horses as food, not as warriors' mounts.

"They approach like foxes, fight like lions, and disappear like birds," said a Frenchman who'd seen Indians in action. Their favorite tactic was the ambush or predawn raid, when people are least watchful. The idea was to hit hard, kill quickly, and escape with prisoners while the enemy was still off balance.

If the enemy put up a strong defense, the braves broke off the fight and made tracks for home. Running away wasn't cowardice but common sense, to the Indian. The warrior's basic rule was simple: Never—*never*—take needless risks. Although there were many woodland tribes, each had only a few hundred warriors. A slain warrior meant one less protector of the tribe, one less hunter to feed it. Every life was precious, not to be wasted in mass charges, battles against long odds, or fights to the finish. When outnumbered or up against a determined enemy, the tribesman escaped. There was no shame in fleeing. Courage, the Indians knew, isn't the same as going out of your way to get hurt. That is stupidity.

Warriors looked forward to taking enemy scalps, and the more scalps the better. Scalping was an ancient custom in North America. Indians believed that the hair was full of magical power. A person's spirit or soul was supposed to be concentrated in the hair at the top of the head. Taking that hair was a way of capturing an enemy's soul and preventing it from haunting the killer as a ghost. It was also proof of courage, without which nobody would believe the brave's war stories. People expected a brave to boast about his victories. Taking many scalps brought respect, made him a desirable husband and someone of importance in the community.

The scalp lock was a warrior's badge of honor and a way of daring enemies to attack him. If a warrior lost a fight, the victor grabbed his scalp lock with one hand and cut a circle around it with a knife. A quick jerk brought it away from the skull in one piece. The scalp was then dried on a frame and hung as a decoration on the warrior's belt.

Scalping wasn't the same as killing. One might be scalped

and live, bald, to tell the tale. But life for the scalped Indian could never be the same. He became officially dead, an outcast among his own people, for he had lost his soul.

Indian captives had their hands tied behind their backs with rawhide thongs, which the Mohawk called "slave straps." To encourage them to move quickly, they were whipped, burned, and bitten. Anyone who lagged behind had his skull split with a tomahawk. Only the strongest survived—something they might soon regret.

When the war party neared home, runners went ahead to announce that it had prisoners. Their news sent everyone streaming out of the village, whooping and laughing. As they left, they picked up heavy sticks and thorny branches.

The prisoners, meanwhile, had been stripped naked even in midwinter. Moments later they saw the "welcoming committee." The villagers had formed a double line, each facing the other, with a narrow aisle in between; the prisoners were to "run the gauntlet." One by one they dashed down the aisle, blows raining on them every step of the way. Those who fell, and many did, were killed and their bodies thrown to the dogs.

The survivors, bruised and bloody, were hauled before the tribal council. Any woman who'd lost a relative for any reason could ask for a prisoner to take his place. The lucky person was bathed in a stream, adopted into the tribe, and became a cherished member of his new family. In this way, tribes kept strong by replacing lost members with people from the outside. Perhaps one-third of the Five Nations were adopted outsiders. They hunted, fought, married, and had children as if they'd been born into their tribes.

Women had the last word about a prisoner's fate. Anyone who wasn't adopted, or who displeased their mistress, knew what to expect. Prolonged, painful death.

Slowly, so as to draw out the agony, the captive was tortured. The women were usually the chief torturers; children were expected to take part to prepare them for adulthood. They stabbed their victim with torches, passing the flames back and forth over his body. They scalped him and poured hot cinders over the raw wounds. His bones were broken one by one, fingers twisted off, and nose, ears, and lips hacked off. Now and then the torturers let him rest to regain his strength before continuing. Often they fed him, gave him water to drink, and allowed him to catch his breath.

The victim, too, had a part to play in his own dying. Despite the pain, he danced and sang for his tormentors, trying not to cry out; screaming was a sign of weakness and would bring shame to his tribe. Dying bravely under torture proved that he was better than his torturers and, strangely, earned their respect.

The bravest victims were honored by being eaten. Indians believed that a person's bravery came from his blood and that it could be transferred to others. Once the victim was out of his misery, his heart might be roasted and given to the young men and boys to "feed" their courage. The blood might also be drunk or, as in a transfusion, put into boys' veins through cuts. Sometimes the entire body was boiled and served at a feast prepared by the women. Torture and cannibalism seem inhuman to us today. Yet the forest people thought them necessary to their well-being, a vital part of life as they understood it.

Woodland Indians lived lives full of hardship and danger. Yet their lives were also exciting and satisfying, proud and self-respecting. They lived as their ancestors had lived through uncounted centuries. Those whose words have come down to us wanted to continue the ancient life forever.

But that was not to be. For strangers had come from where the sun rises out of the great saltwater, strangers who would change the Indian and his world forever.

AT FIRST, those strangers showed little interest in North America. John Cabot, sailing for the English in 1497, and Giovanni da Verrazano, sailing for France in 1523, were satisfied to cruise along the Atlantic coast and make some crude maps.

Ten years later, the Frenchman Jacques Cartier found the mouth of a mighty river, which he named the St. Lawrence. Sailing upstream, he sent men ashore to ask the Indians where they were. The Indians called the land *Cannata*, an Iroquoian word for a village or settlement. Cartier returned from "Canada" with nothing more valuable than sacks of iron pyrites, "fool's gold."

The first Europeans to find use for the continent came seeking another type of wealth. John Cabot had brought back news that the northern waters teemed with codfish. From the 1490s on, every spring English, French, Dutch, and Portuguese fishermen boarded their flimsy boats and headed for the Grand Banks off Newfoundland, an island near Canada's east coast. Each day they caught tons of cod with simple hand lines. Each night they brought the catch ashore to be dried, salted, and stowed in barrels. As the chill winds of autumn began to blow, they upped anchor for home, before they became icebound for the winter.

Before long, Indians discovered that the visitors had things they needed. They approached the strangers, offering to exchange furs for iron tools and colored cloth. The fishermen jumped at the chance to trade. At this time, fashionable gentlemen in Europe demanded soft, warm fur for making their hats and lining their coats. A few fine pelts, especially beaver pelts, brought more cash than boatloads of salt cod.

When questioned about their pelts, the Indians explained that, fine as they were, better ones were to be found inland. Behind the coast lay lakes and streams swarming with beaver, marten, otter, and other furbearing animals. Better yet, they'd heard from people dwelling around five freshwater "seas" of places rich in shiny yellow metal and stones that sparkled with the colors of the rainbow.

The French decided to get to the bottom of these rumors and, if possible, also find a shortcut to the Far East. Columbus had searched for this shortcut by sailing west, only to find the New World blocking his way. Surely, French explorers reasoned, the St. Lawrence or another river cut through the continent to China and India.

In 1603, Samuel de Champlain made the first of eleven voyages to Canada. He found no gold or river passage to Asia. Yet, in his failure, he became the father of New France, as Canada came to be called. Port Royal, Acadia, was founded in 1605, the first permanent French settlement in the New World.

Three years later, Champlain came to a mammoth rock rising hundreds of feet above the St. Lawrence. The Indians called the place *Kebec*, "Where the Water Narrows." Here Champlain founded Quebec, one of the great cities of the New World, followed in 1611 by Montreal ("Royal Mountain") 120 miles upstream.

The English, meanwhile were taking a close look at the coast farther south. In 1607, ships set 142 settlers ashore at Jamestown, Virginia. After terrible hardships, during which Captain John Smith was saved by Pocahontas, the colony took root and prospered. Other English colonies were founded during the years that followed. The Pilgrims arrived at Plymouth, Massachusetts, in 1620; the Puritans settled in nearby Massachusetts Bay nine years later. Maryland began in 1634. New Amsterdam, taken from the Dutch in 1664, became New York. William Penn founded Pennsylvania in 1682 as a place where Quakers could enjoy religious freedom. Other colonies were founded, and, with the creation of Georgia in 1732, England had thirteen colonies along the Atlantic coast.

The French and English colonies represented opposing

ways of life. New France knew nothing of self-government. The king in Paris appointed the colonial officials, paid them, and spelled out their orders to the last detail. These officials ruled in their master's name, regardless of the settlers' wishes or welfare. For it was the king's right to command, given him by God, and the people's duty to obey.

The settlers, like their country, belonged to the king. He brought them across the ocean at his own expense, granted each a plot of land, a gun, some ammunition, farm tools, two pigs, six hens, and a cock. They even owed him their mates. During the early days of New France, the king sent shiploads of unmarried girls to become brides of the lonely settlers.

The people were mostly illiterate, with neither books nor newspapers to trouble their thoughts. New France hadn't a single printing press. Its one college, in Quebec, trained only priests.

New France existed for two reasons: to serve God and to make the king rich. There, as in most European countries, one's religion wasn't a private matter. Kings decided their people's religion, and those who couldn't go along with their decisions suffered for their beliefs. If they were lucky, they only had to pay higher taxes and were refused many kinds of jobs. If unlucky, they might be jailed, tortured, and burned alive.

France was a Roman Catholic country, and so New France was Roman Catholic as well. The French believed that God wanted them to make Roman Catholics out of the Indians. Priests, called "black robes" by the Indians, traveled everywhere on foot and by canoe to bring their religion to the tribes. Often, at first, the Indians tortured them to death for their efforts. The Five Nations and the Huron were especially cruel to priests. Yet for every priest killed, another came forward to take his place. Gradually they converted hundreds of tribesmen, gathering these "praying Indians" into separate villages. Although now Roman Catholics, the Indians kept to their old way of life, following the warpath whenever they pleased.

The cross and the white lily flag of France dominate this village of "praying Indians." French missionaries were very active in converting Indians to Christianity and using them against their English enemies. From Vetromile, The Abnakis *(1866).*

New France also existed to fill the king's treasure chests. Settlers had been sent not to cultivate the land and live on it, but to further the fur trade. Canadian farmers seldom grew enough to feed the white population; without food shipments from home, the colony would have starved in most years. Manufactured goods of all types had to come across the ocean, since they weren't made in the colony.

The fur trade, New France's only source of wealth, was carried on with the king's permission and for his profit. Every time a beaver pelt was sold in France, the king's tax collector put out his hand for the royal share.

The pioneers of the fur trade were adventurers called *coureurs de bois,* "runners of the forest." A young man bored with farm work, or a soldier itching for action, took off to seek his fortune in Indian country. It was a hard life, one that would keep him in the wilderness for at least a year at a time, often two or three.

Kneeling in an overloaded canoe, pipes stuck between their teeth, he and his companions paddled for two hours at a stretch; they calculated time by the number of pipes smoked between stops. A good team paddled forty-eight strokes a minute, sending the birchbark canoe shooting across the water. If the waterway was blocked or if they had to get from one waterway to another, they "portaged"—carried the canoe and its contents around the blockage or overland to the next river or lake, sometimes a distance of several miles. When it rained, they sheltered beneath the upturned canoe, propping it up by stones at either end. When they ran out of salt bacon and corn cakes, they chewed their leather moccasins and jackets, or nibbled the bark of trees, until something better came their way.

Coureurs de bois learned to live, speak, and *think* like Indians; otherwise, they learned the meaning of pain at the hands of skilled torturers. Despite dangers and hardship, they loved the free life of the forest. No sooner did they sell their pelts at Montreal than they bought fresh supplies and returned to the woods as quickly as possible. These men were the backbone of New France's prosperity.

How different was the picture of the English colonies! The only bond between the thirteen colonies was their loyalty *(so far)* to the king; otherwise, they were like separate countries forever squabbling about boundaries, trade, and defense. Each had its elected assembly, whose members demanded their rights as Englishmen. In most colonies, they also argued with the royal governor, especially over his salary, which they paid. The Five Nations were more united than the thirteen colonies.

The average English settler didn't care about the fur trade one way or another. The best hunting grounds were around the westernmost Great Lakes, beyond the towering Appalachian Mountains, a roadless wilderness. The St. Lawrence, however, gave the French a direct highway to the interior.

English people were more interested in owning and making a living from the land. They grew everything they needed, selling the remainder in Europe. Tobacco, cotton, timber, and indigo— a purple dye—brought high prices overseas. Although they were forbidden to export manufactured goods, they could make anything for their own use. Colonists wore clothes of American-made cloth, lived in houses built of American-made bricks, and furnished them with American-made furniture. Whatever they were unable to make at home had to be brought from England, regardless of the cost, for the colonies could not buy anything not made in the mother country, even if it sold at a lower price.

English colonists were better educated than Canadians. Each colony had its own newspapers, and most had colleges to train doctors and lawyers in addition to clergymen. Except for a handful of Roman Catholics and Jews, settlers belonged to various Protestant churches.

EUROPEANS AND INDIANS influenced each other in many ways. Each people took from the other and gave them something in return.

Whites borrowed heavily from Indians. The names of places, common things, and animals were taken over from Indian languages, mostly Algonquian. Among these are: *hickory, skunk, moose, chipmunk, raccoon, woodchuck, opossum, terrapin,* and *musketoe* (mosquito). Indian foods such as the potato, tomato, corn, maple sugar, wild rice, and lobster are today known worldwide. Nearly two hundred drugs still used in the United States were discovered by Indians, mostly woodlanders. This list included herbs to stop bleeding, ease the pains of childbirth, and prevent death from rattlesnake bites. A soup of boiled tobacco leaves is a powerful insecticide when smeared on the body. Colonists often preferred "Indian doctors" to their own physicians.

Indians, on the other hand, eagerly took whatever the whites had to make their lives easier. Needles, thread, kettles, and cloth were prized everywhere. Cloth, unlike animal skins, came in summer and winter weights, in colors bright as the rainbow's, and was easy to sew; best of all, a squaw didn't have to soften it by chewing on it.

Whites made the Indian's own weapons better than any tribesman could. Iron arrowheads cut deeper than flint and saved hours of labor in making. Iron scalping knives were ordinary wooden-handled butcher knives. Iron tomahawks were mass-produced. Lighter and sharper than anything the Indians knew, their handles were often hollow, leading to a pipe bowl mounted over the blade; thus, a brave could enjoy a smoke between battles. And nothing the Indian had could match the musket's range and killing power.

Most of all, the Indian demanded alcohol. He had an uncontrolable craving for liquor, the Frenchman's brandy and the Englishman's rum. Liquor became the curse of Indian life. White traders deliberately got tribesmen drunk in order to cheat them out of their furs. Often a whole year's catch, hundreds of pelts, was exchanged for a few quarts of cheap liquor.

Unlike whites, who usually drank to be sociable and to feel good, the Indian *always* drank to get drunk. Being drunk might give him visions in which he believed he saw and spoke to the nature spirits. It puffed up his pride and he became a giant, fearless and to be feared.

He also became a killer. Drunken braves burned their homes and murdered their families. A traveler described the panic that spread through a village when liquor casks were opened: "We soon saw the Indian women and their children skulking in the ... bushes, for fear of the intoxicated Indians, who were drinking deeper. The women were [hiding] guns, hatchets, and every deadly or dangerous weapon, that murder or harm might not be the consequence."

Indians became "hooked" on the white man's goods. Growing to depend upon them, they couldn't live without them. They would do anything to get fresh supplies. As a result, they overhunted, killing more and more beaver until the rodents vanished from certain areas. They also fought other Indians. During the 1640s, the Five Nations nearly exterminated the Huron to capture their share of the fur trade.

And, worst of all, the whites began to draw the Indian into their own struggles. Thus he became a pawn in a bloody game he couldn't win.

✤≫ II ≪✤

Three Wars

THE WORLD of the 1600s and 1700s was a violent place. European nations were constantly at war over issues that still trouble us today. Where should a boundary line be drawn? Who should rule a neighboring territory? What nation has a better right to this seaport or to that province? Answers to these questions were found, as they still are, on battlefields during long and costly wars.

These wars, however, weren't fought only on the soil of the Old World. If nations had fleets, their struggles ranged across the seven seas. If they had colonies, the settlers were expected to fight for the interests of the mother country.

The most serious wars involved France and England. France's King Louis XIV was an ambitious, arrogant ruler determined to dominate Europe with his armies. King William III of England was equally determined to stop him. He would make any alliance, pay any price, to defeat France. This was no empty threat, for, in 1689, England and its allies began the War of the Grand Alliance, known in America as King William's War.

France was ready for any struggle in the New World. The

English colonists, everyone knew, outnumbered the French by at least 15 to 1. (In 1750, there were 1,200,000 English as compared to 80,000 French settlers.) Yet numbers don't tell the whole story. For the English colonies were disunited, each following its own policies, while the Canadians were a unified people. Like the fingers of a clenched fist, they needed only their king's command to strike hard blows.

New France could also count on Indian support. The Canadians always got along well with the Algonquian tribes and the Huron. Patient and understanding, they earned the Indians' friendship. Since the Canadians' main concern was the fur trade, they had no need to take the land or change it. Except for small farms near their settlements, they left the land as they found it, wild and unfenced. The canoes of the *coureurs de bois* carved only ripples in the waterways as they passed.

Young Canadians often "went native," becoming Indians in all but name. *Coureurs de bois,* even army officers, lived with squaws; their children, part Indian, part white, were known as "half-breeds."

Not the English. Except for the Pennsylvania Quakers, who treated Indians fairly and were never attacked, Englishmen despised them as savages. The Indians, for their part, thought the English selfish and greedy, with no respect for nature. With ax and plow, the English ruined the forest, slashed open the ground, and enclosed the fields with stone or rail fences. The game animals, whose spirits allowed humans to enjoy wholesome meat, were exterminated or driven away.

So were the Indians. The northern tribes from Acadia to Lake Superior knew about the English. And what they knew, they didn't like. The English had made scores of treaties with the coastal tribes, but in the end broke them all. If the Indians had land that the English wanted, the English would lie, and cheat, and kill to get it. The Virginians and New Englanders had burned crops to starve Indian villagers. Tribesmen might kill one

The Indians resented the English for, as in this settlement, they cleared the forest and fenced in the land wherever they settled. This picture is from Campbell's Travels in the Interior Parts of North America *(London, 1793).*

another; they'd never deliberately destroy nature's bounty, because such waste was sinful. Distant tribes knew how the English had attacked sleeping villages and massacred their inhabitants. During the Pequot War of 1637, the Puritans surrounded and set fire to an Indian village on the Mystic River in Connecticut. Those who weren't burned immediately died in a hail of bullets as they ran through the flames.

When the French Canadians later went among the Indians with red tomahawks and black wampum, brandy and muskets, the Indians readily took to the warpath against the English. Praying Indians also joined, led often by their priests. Missionaries were busy in hundreds of villages, teaching the people to love God and hate the English. A chief of the Abnaki of Maine, one of the fiercest Algonquian peoples, learned that the Virgin Mary was a Frenchwoman. Her son, Jesus, had been crucified by Protestant Englishmen, and all who wished to join Him in heaven must earn their place by slaying His enemies. We think today that what these priests did was wrong. But in looking at the past, we must remember that people acted according to *their* beliefs, not ours. Priests who joined war parties really believed that they were serving God.

Champlain defeats warriors of the Five Nations near Ticonderoga, July 30, 1609. This battle, which made firm allies of the Canadian Indians, turned the Five Nations against the French for the next century and a half. From Champlain's Life and Travels *(1613).*

Only the Five Nations were friendly to the English. They, too, had long memories. And they remembered that summer of 1609, when Samuel de Champlain led a war party of Huron and others to the shore of Lake Champlain, named in his own honor. To win the Hurons' loyalty, he'd decided to help them against their enemies. Champlain fired into a group of Mohawk who, never having seen muskets, ran away, leaving several dead, including two sachems. That small victory would cost thousands of French lives during the next two and a half centuries.

The Five Nations never forgot, or forgave, Champlain's action. They befriended the English, sticking with them through thick and thin until the American Revolution. Sometimes they fought side by side; at other times they stood aside, letting the English fight on their own. But they never betrayed them, never let them down. No one can say if their friendship guaranteed England's victory in the struggle for North America. But this much is certain: Had the Five Nations joined the French, England would have been driven from the continent. Then there wouldn't have been a United States of America as we know it.

FRANCE HOPED to use King William's War to destroy the English colonies. And Louis de Buade, Comte de Frontenac, governor of New France, was just the man for the job. Although seventy years old and growing frail, he was still full of fire and fight. Frontenac had been fighting ever since becoming a soldier at the age of fifteen. His ability and good luck were legendary. Always in the thick of the battle, with comrades dropping around him, his

Count Frontenac was a fierce old soldier who sometimes put on a breechclout and moccasins and did the war dance with friendly Indians. This is a photograph of a statue of the count.

worst wound had been a broken arm. Eventually he became a general and one of Louis XIV's most trusted officers.

Frontenac's plan called for invading the English colonies with fifteen hundred Canadians and swarms of Indians. Moving south from Montreal and Quebec, he would capture the city of New York and key points in New England. No mercy would be shown to the defeated. All Protestants were to be expelled, except for workers with needed skills, who would be kept as slaves. Their property would be given to settlers brought from Canada and France. Fortunately for the colonists, Frontenac's plans were upset when ships with supplies and reinforcements failed to arrive from France.

Frontenac, however, was no quitter. If he couldn't mount a full-scale invasion, he'd sting the colonies with *la petite guerre*—"the little war" or guerrilla warfare. In the *coureurs de bois* he had perfect guerrilla troops, experts in the Indians' hit-and-run tactics, and he intended to use them.

Frontenac began the war early in 1690. Three war parties made up of praying Indians and *coureurs de bois* lanced deep into New England and New York. Their mission was not to seize territory, but to keep the enemy off balance, always fearful, always wondering where the next blow would fall. Their weapon was to be terror, the deliberate harming of civilians to spread panic among the English.

The first war party headed for Albany, New York, a large town near the junction of the Hudson and Mohawk rivers. It was rough going. After crossing the frozen St. Lawrence, the raiders were caught in a snowstorm. Traveling on foot, each man carried his supplies on his back or pulled them on a sledge, a wooden platform resembling a large ski. They arrived in the Albany area so exhausted that they decided to go after a less dangerous target. On February 8, 1690, they wiped out Schenectady in a predawn attack.

The next month, another war party slipped out of the woods

near Salmon Falls, New Hampshire. It was Schenectady all over again. This time, thirty-four died and fifty-four were taken prisoner. The captives—those who survived the horrors of the northward march—were held in Canada until their families or the colonial government exchanged them for ransom. Most eventually returned home. Many others, as we'll see, stayed behind to become white Indians.

Frontenac's third war party was made up of five hundred Christian Abnaki and Canadians. On May 27, 1690, it struck Fort Loyal at Casco Bay, Maine, where the city of Portland now stands. The tiny fort was no match for such a powerful force. After holding out for four days, the fort's commander, Captain Sylvanus Davis, asked for surrender terms. Baron de Portneuf, the French commander, swore "by the great and everlasting God" that everyone would be treated kindly and allowed to go to an English settlement nearby. The colonists had only to lay down their weapons and all would be well, he promised.

He lied.

The gates of Fort Loyal swung open, and the people began to file out, unarmed. As they did, the Abnaki let out bloodcurdling war whoops and leaped upon them. Tomahawks flashed. Braves danced about with dripping scalps raised high. About a hundred colonists died on the spot or were taken prisoner. Portneuf and his officers stood by calmly, saying little and doing less to stop the slaughter.

Frontenac's war parties of 1690 began a reign of terror unheard of in North America. Indians had raided settlements and killed their inhabitants before. But now, for the first time, whites led them in massacring other whites. It was an evil omen for the future.

These raids sent a shiver of horror through New York and New England. The Reverend Cotton Mather of Boston reminded Massachusetts militiamen about Fort Loyal. The enemy, he said, his voice rising, ". . . have horribly Murdered . . . scores

of your dear Country-men, whose Blood cries in your Ears.
. . . Vengeance, Dear Country-men! Vengeance upon our Murderers!"
Mather's cry would echo across the English colonies for the next
seventy years.

Frontenac was mistaken if he thought that the English
would sit still while he destroyed them bit by bit. New York
called out the militia, units of volunteer citizen-soldiers, to defend
its settlements. Massachusetts prepared to carry the war into the
heart of Canada. The other colonies, however, did nothing, as if
they were watching the struggle from the safety of a distant
galaxy.

Massachusetts appointed forty-year-old William Phips to
lead its forces. "Lucky Billy," folks called him, and nobody deserved that nickname better than he. Born in poverty, Billy, a
ship's carpenter by trade, moved to Boston as a young man.
There he wooed a wealthy widow, married her, and used her
fortune to make his own in shipbuilding and trade. His luck and
his fortune grew with the years. He once salvaged tons of gold,
silver, and jewels from a Spanish treasure ship sunk off the Ba-
hama Islands.

Lucky Billy knew as much about making war as did most
New Englanders; that is, very little indeed. But since there was
a job to be done, and since English troops couldn't be spared from
Europe, he'd have to learn quickly. In any case, he felt that his
luck would make up for his ignorance. And it did, for a while.

In May 1690, Phips led seven hundred men in fourteen small
ships to Port Royal, Acadia, in southeastern Canada. That port
had become a base for privateers—privately owned ships licensed
by Louis XIV to attack English merchantmen. Hundreds of vessels, many of them from Boston, had been taken, their cargoes
seized, and their crews held for ransom.

Lucky Billy made short work of this privateers' nest. He
attacked it, captured it, and made its people swear allegiance to
the king of England. The expedition cost Massachusetts no lives

and paid for itself with loot from Port Royal's warehouses and churches.

Phips's victory encouraged him to think grand thoughts. Surely, if Port Royal fell so easily, taking Quebec shouldn't be all *that* difficult. The Massachusetts Assembly agreed and voted money for another—larger—expedition.

Lucky Billy arrived before Quebec in October 1690, with three thousand men aboard thirty-five ships, three of which had been supplied by the New York colony. Frontenac was waiting for them with about fifteen hundred men on the heights above the St. Lawrence.

The colonists stood open mouthed, staring at the city atop the cliffs. The problem with Quebec was that ships can't float themselves up cliff sides. To take the city, troops must be landed and climb the cliffs, straight into the muzzles of the defenders' cannon.

Phips, still counting on his luck, sent a messenger to demand Frontenac's surrender. The old lion growled: "I have no reply to make to your general other than from the mouths of my cannon and muskets." After some landing of troops on the riverbank and popping of guns to test Quebec's defenses, the fleet sailed for home. Lucky Billy's luck had run out, though time would prove that he'd been on the right track. Quebec, as he realized, was the key to Canada. As long as the French held it, they would keep a firm foothold in North America. Once they lost it, however, they would be swept off the continent as surely as tomorrow's sunrise.

In the meantime, King William's War dragged on. With neither side strong enough to deliver the knockout blow, there was nothing left to do but continue with border raids. Both sides played a vicious game. *Coureurs de bois* and Christian Indians came south, while the Five Nations visited New France with torch and tomahawk.

During these raids, women on both sides proved that they

could be as courageous as any man. One day, warriors of the Five Nations met their match in Madeleine de Verchères, a Canadian girl of fourteen. Madeleine lived with her parents in a farming village near Montreal. She was attending to her chores when a war party crept up, and, while some braves surprised the farmers in the fields, others went for the stockade.

Madeleine saw them coming and ran toward the stockade, a brave close on her heels. Just as he reached out to grab her long hair, she slammed the gate in his face. Six people in the stockade now stood against the angry braves. In addition to Madeleine, there were her brothers, aged ten and twelve, an old man, and two militiamen. The militiamen panicked, trying first to hide and then to escape, which would have meant certain death. Fortunately, Madeleine had enough courage for them all. She made everyone go up to the firing platform and, by her example, encouraged them to hold out until help arrived a few days later.

Mrs. Hannah Dustin's adventure has become part of New England folklore. Hannah lived with her husband Thomas and their seven children in Haverhill, Massachusetts, thirty miles north of Boston. Haverhill was frontier country in 1697, and the Dustin children, aged two to seventeen, were expected to do their share of the farm work. On March 3, they were helping their father in the fields. Hannah, who'd given birth to her eighth child the week before, was resting in bed at home. Mary Neff, a neighbor, had come to help with the baby and the housework for a couple of days.

No one saw the painted Abnaki darting from tree to tree. They had been hunting nearby and decided that Haverhill was too tempting a target to bypass. The townspeople didn't realize their danger until it was too late. The Indians struck, killed, scalped, and left the village in flames.

Mr. Dustin was torn between saving his loved ones at home or those with him in the fields. He couldn't do both, for the Abnaki were already rushing across the fields. He chose to save

Thomas Dustin keeps the Indians at bay, allowing his children to escape to safety in a fortified house nearby.

the children. As they ran to safety in a farmhouse used as a makeshift fort, he covered them with his musket. He must have been a good shot, for the braves dove for cover and stayed there.

Hannah was dozing when Mary's screams jarred her awake. Suddenly there were shouts, followed by the smashing of glass and the cracking of wood. The Abnaki burst into the bedroom, waving bloody tomahawks. One tore the blanket from the bed; another dragged Hannah out, together with the infant. Still wearing her nightgown, without shoes on her feet, they hustled her and Mary out of the house and into the woods.

They were moving quickly when Hannah's baby began to cry. A brave, fearful that it might give away their location, snatched it from her arms. Paralyzed with fear, unwilling to believe her eyes, she watched him whirl it by the feet, smashing its head against a tree. From that moment on she burned for revenge.

The women were driven deeper into the forest until they came to the Abnaki's camp. Other prisoners were already there, some of whom were tomahawked when they seemed too weak to travel. Hannah, Mary, and an English boy were given to a family of two braves, three squaws, and seven children. They then broke camp, each family going its own way to avoid detection.

The next six weeks were hell for the captives. Cold and hungry, their frostbitten feet bleeding, they were driven northward toward Canada. At night, while the Indians slept snugly around a campfire, they huddled on the fringes beyond its warmth. The Abnaki never tied them, because there was no place to run in the midst of the forest. Besides, the captives knew the penalty for trying to escape: slow death by torture.

As they lay down on the night of April 29, Hannah whispered her plan to the others. She meant to kill their captors in their sleep.

The sky was purpling in the east when the three whites rose and, finding tomahawks near a woodpile, stood over the sleeping figures. The grieving mother gave the signal.

Ten times the tomahawks rose and fell, smashing into the Indians' brains. All died instantly, except for a wounded squaw and a boy who ran screaming into the woods. Calmly the whites scalped the corpses, took whatever supplies they needed, and headed home. The Massachusetts Assembly promptly gave them £50, a fortune to farmer folk, for their grisly trophies. The colonists considered the money well spent.

Hatred bred hatred. Violence called forth more violence. If Frontenac sent Indians against defenseless settlements, settlers felt justified in offering bounties for Indian scalps. Indians loyal to France had a price on their heads. A brave's scalp brought so much; scalps of squaws, the elderly, and children were worth proportionately less.

Professional bounty hunters set out with musket and scalping knife to make their fortunes. For many years, their handiwork was displayed in the courthouse of Salem, Massachusetts, the same building in which the famous witch trials were held. Nailed to the wall, for all to see and touch, were row upon row of Indian scalps. Bounty hunters could also be seen parading the streets of New York and New England towns wearing wigs made of scalps.

King William's War ended in September 1697, with a peace treaty signed at Ryswick, the Netherlands. Eight years of fighting had changed little in Europe. In America, where all captured territory was returned, nothing changed, except for those who had suffered. It is impossible to count the war's victims, for rec-

Mrs. Dustin prepares to tomahawk the Indians who killed her child and kidnapped her and two others from Haverhill, Massachusetts. Picture from Bryant's Popular History of the United States *(1897).*

ords weren't kept. At most, two thousand people—English, French, Indians—lost their lives.

THE TREATY OF RYSWICK was merely a truce allowing the European powers to prepare for another, much bigger, conflict. The aim of that conflict was to prevent Louis XIV's grandson, the Duke of Anjou, from becoming king of Spain. England and the Netherlands especially feared that this would give Louis XIV control of Western Europe, threatening their own independence. The war that began in 1702 lasted eleven years. Europeans knew it as the War of the Spanish Succession. The English colonists named it for Queen Anne, who took the throne after William III's death.

Queen Anne's War was a stalemate from the beginning. With France and England spilling rivers of blood on European battlefields, no troops could be spared for North America. The colonists would have to fight it out by themselves.

The Marquis Pierre de Vaudreuil, Frontenac's successor as governor of New France, made a wise decision early in the war. Vaudreuil feared the Five Nations and was eager to keep them on the sidelines. As a result, he offered them a truce, promising not to invade New York so long as the English didn't threaten Canada from that direction. The sachems agreed, thus forcing the New York English to keep still or lose the Indians' friendship.

Vaudreuil's truce allowed him to concentrate on New England. Once again, bands of Indians and *coureurs de bois* swept southward, spreading terror wherever they appeared. One of these raids became, for Americans, the most famous incident of Queen Anne's War.

That incident concerns the Williams family of Deerfield, Massachusetts, a farming community of three hundred on the Connecticut River, the colony's western border. Deerfield was what Boonesborough, Kentucky, would be a century later: the last outpost of English civilization. Beyond it lay the virgin wilderness filled with mystery and danger.

Reverend John Williams lived in Deerfield with his wife, Eunice and their eight children. Williams, the village minister, was a ramrod-stiff Puritan who taught his children to work hard, thank God for their blessings, and not complain about misfortune. It was stern teaching, but it prepared them for the ordeal that lay ahead.

In the cold darkness of February 29, 1704, Williams was jolted awake by shouts and the sound of his front door caving in under the blows of axes. Automatically, his head still fuzzy with sleep, he grabbed a pistol and aimed at a figure near his bed.

Luckily the gun misfired. His target was an Indian chief whose death would have meant death for Williams's entire family. The chief belonged to a raiding party of 250 Frenchmen, Abnaki, and Caughnawaga, Christian Mohawks who had moved to Canada from New York. They had traveled all the way from Montreal on snowshoes, buffeted by gusty winds that took away their breath. On the day before the attack, they reached the forest on Deerfield's outskirts. Numb with cold and fatigue, but not daring to make a fire for fear of being seen, they scooped burrows in the snow, lined them with spruce bows, and tried to hide from the wind.

Luck was with them. Toward morning they were able to climb into the village without being seen, thanks to the wind-blown snow that had piled against the stockade. They took Deerfield quickly, although not before losing 40 men; the minister's neighbors' guns worked better than his own.

The Williams family was in a state of shock when the youngest, a boy of six, and a Negro woman servant were taken outside and killed on the doorstep. We don't know the reason for this double murder. All we can say is that Indians on the warpath were unpredictable. Often they behaved in ways that colonists

Indians attack a farmhouse during the Deerfield massacre. This picture is from the 1833 edition of the Reverend Williams's book, The Redeemed Captive Returning to Zion. *Indians liked to time their attacks for the early morning hours, when their victims were least alert.*

then, and students today, couldn't understand. The rest of the Williams family was told to dress and be ready to travel at sunup.

One hundred twelve captives began the trek to Canada, of whom 17 were killed along the way. A man was killed when the Indians got drunk on rum taken in Deerfield. Crying infants had their brains dashed out against trees. Anyone unable to keep up the pace was tomahawked, including Mrs. Williams.

Killing the weak was kindness, not cruelty, in the Indians' eyes; they would have wanted the same for themselves and their loved ones in a similar situation. A weakened person unable to travel in the wilderness could either be killed to be put out of his or her misery or left to a slow death from cold and hunger. Nobody wanted to face the gleaming fangs and blazing eyes of timber wolves.

Captives who reached Canada were treated kindly. Governor Vaudreuil spent his own money to buy them from the Indians, holding them until ransom money arrived from Massachusetts. During the next two years, most Deerfield captives returned to their homes. The village built Reverend Williams a new house; he remarried and added five more children to his flock. He described his family's ordeal in *The Redeemed Captive Returning to Zion,* a book widely read in the colonies in the 1700s.

Yet the Williams's story doesn't end here. The minister's seven-year-old daughter, also named Eunice, discovered that Indians had a gentler nature than anyone had supposed. She and the

The trail of tears. English captives, their hands bound behind their backs, set out on the long winter's journey to Canada. Those who weakened were killed so as not to slow up the march.

younger Deerfield children (those who didn't cry) made the journey to Canada on the backs or in the arms of braves. Although the others were ransomed, Eunice was taken to the Caughnawaga's village and put into a Catholic school. She became a Catholic and, in time, married the brave who'd carried her through the snow. The minister's daughter became a squaw, lived in a wigwam, and had two half-breed children. Years later she visited Deerfield three times with her husband and children. Her father was dead by then, but her relatives welcomed her warmly. When the visits ended, no one tried to keep her or to talk her out of returning to Canada. For her life was now in the north country. She had become a white Indian.

Eunice Williams was one of many captives who came to accept the Indians and live among them. Thousands of whites became Indians over the years, while few if any Indians chose the whites' way of life.

Woodlanders, as we've seen, were anxious to adopt outsiders into their tribes. It made no difference whether these outsiders were fellow Indians or whites, so long as they replaced relatives who had died. In the southern colonies and Spanish America, escaped Negro slaves were adopted: Indians knew nothing of racial discrimination.

Children were particularly welcome, and the younger the better, since they would easily forget their real parents. Soon after capture, children and parents were separated. Those selected for adoption were treated well. Good treatment wasn't just an act, because the Indians already regarded them as fellow tribesmen. A Pennsylvania boy captured when he was four recalled how a squaw calmed his fears, accepting him as her son:

The last I remember of my mother she was running, carrying me in her arms. Suddenly she fell to the ground on her face, and I was taken from her. Overwhelmed with fright, I knew nothing

*more until I opened my eyes to find myself in the lap of an
Indian woman. Looking kindly down into my face, she smiled on
me and gave me some dried deer's meat and maple sugar. From
that hour I believed she loved me as a mother. I am sure I
returned to her the affection of a son.*

Older children were adopted in a ceremony lasting several
hours. First, they were hit lightly on the back to "beat the white-
ness" out of them. Second, they were dunked in a stream and
scrubbed with sand to wash it off. They were then dressed in
Indian clothes, given belts of wampum, and had their faces
painted with red stripes. From that moment on they were Indians, accepted by their tribe and treated as equals in every way.

Girls learned the squaw's work from their new mothers.
Boys were toughened by their new fathers and uncles to prepare
them for the hunting trail and the warpath. John McCullough,
taken at the age of eight, remembered how his uncle trained him:

*In the beginning of winter, he used to raise me by daylight every
morning and make me sit down in the creek up to my chin in the
cold water, in order to make me hardy as he said, whilst he would
sit on the bank smoking his pipe until he thought I had been long
enough in the water. He would then bid me to dive. After I came
out of the water he would order me not to go near the fire until I
would be dry. I was kept at that till the water was frozen over.
He would then break the ice for me and send me in as before.*

Little John wasn't happy with such treatment, but he didn't
hate it, either. It made him strong and proud that he'd stood up
to it "with the firmness of an Indian." He also knew that he could
marry anyone he chose, even another white captive, and become
a chief if he earned the honor.

Apart from raids and prisoner taking, Queen Anne's War

seemed to be going nowhere. Its only military victory and its worst disaster belonged to the English. Both took place in Canada.

The victory came after two unsuccessful attempts to capture Port Royal. In July 1710, a squadron of thirty New England ships aided by five British men-of-war forced the French garrison to surrender. The town was renamed Annapolis Royal—"Anne's Royal Town"—in the queen's honor. Since it was the area's only stronghold, all of Acadia fell into English hands with one blow.

Queen Anne's military advisers decided to follow up this victory with an assault on Quebec the next year. Every warship and redcoat that could be spared from Europe was sent across the Atlantic. Where Billy Phips had failed, surely, they thought, Her Majesty's own forces would succeed.

Toward evening, August 22, 1711, Admiral Sir Hovenden Walker's flagship, the *Edgar,* nosed into the Gulf of St. Lawrence near Anticosti Island, where the river meets the sea. Behind him eight warships led seventy transports crammed with twelve thousand soldiers, sailors, marines, and New England volunteers.

Governor Vaudreuil himself couldn't have picked a better man to lead the enemy fleet. Admiral Walker, bumbling and cranky, never listened to advice; it was an insult to him if anyone even made a suggestion. Officers kept their distance, terrified of his temper tantrums. Right or wrong, Walker wanted things done his way, and no questions asked.

That night a fog blanketed the Gulf of St. Lawrence. A storm blew up, making the ships bob and toss like so many corks. Walker lost his bearings and mistook the gulf's northern for its southern shore. Even today, seamen dread the cliffs and rocky shallows of the northern shore. The southern shore, though no snug harbor, is less treacherous.

The admiral hoisted lanterns to signal the fleet to head north and then went to bed. An hour later, an officer woke him to report the rumbling of breakers ahead. Walker barked something about idiotic officers questioning their superiors and went back to bed.

Another officer, very excited, woke him with the same story. The admiral cursed his rudeness, but came up on deck in his nightshirt and slippers. Over the rumbling of the waves he heard the crunching of wood and the screams of men as ten ships smashed against the rocks. Nearly a thousand English bodies washed up on the beach in the days that followed. Walker lost heart and returned home in disgrace.

No fleets or armies were sent to North America after 1711. It was otherwise in Europe, where the Duke of Marlborough led England's armies to stunning victories. Louis XIV, old and bankrupt, decided that he'd had enough of war. In April 1713, he accepted a peace treaty signed at Utrecht in the Netherlands. When he died two years later, his last words were: "I have loved war too much." He'd never spoken truer words.

Although Louis's grandson was recognized as king of Spain, he couldn't inherit the crown of France as well. In America, Louis gave England Acadia, the island of Newfoundland, and the region bordering Hudson Bay. In addition to the men drowned off Anticosti Island, about 250 New Englanders and Canadians lost their lives. Indian losses are unknown. Tens of thousands of soldiers died in European battles.

THE TREATY OF UTRECHT kept the peace for thirty-one years. But it was an uneasy peace. Although the guns were stilled, bad feelings between France and England ran deep. Each distrusted the other. Each feared the other's power and intentions. Few doubted that, one way or another, war would flare up once again.

The loss of Acadia had put New France in a dangerous position. Imagine Acadia and Newfoundland as a pair of jaws with the Gulf of St. Lawrence between them. The English bull-dog had only to snap its jaws shut to cut New France's lifeline. Furs are valuable, but they can't be baked into bread or made into gunpowder. Without supplies from overseas, the colony was doomed.

But there was a way out—put a big "rock" in the bulldog's jaws to keep them open. France still owned Cape Breton Island commanding the entrance to the Gulf of St. Lawrence. In 1720, the new king, Louis XV, ordered work begun on a fortress to guard this key spot. Not only would the fortress keep the St. Lawrence open, it could shelter privateers. Once again, New Englanders grew anxious as they gazed out over the stormy Atlantic.

The fortress, named Louisbourg—"Louis's Town"—in the king's honor was actually three separate fortresses placed so as to reinforce one another. The main position was a walled town built on a peninsula facing the Atlantic on one side and a large harbor on the other. Looming above the town, as if growing out of it, was the citadel, or fort. Shaped like a five-pointed star, the citadel was designed to catch attackers in a crossfire the moment they came between any two points. Stone walls thirty feet high and ten feet thick had gun ports for 148 heavy cannon, trained mostly on the coast and harbor. On the town's land side, an invader faced a different set of defenses. The walls there overlooked a plain with not so much as a twig to hide behind. A ditch eighty feet wide and twelve feet deep scarred the ground beyond the walls. Swivel guns, small cannon easily turned in any direction and firing chunks of scrap iron, covered the approaches to the walls.

Four thousand people—innkeepers, craftsmen, traders, women, and children—lived in the town, in addition to the seven hundred soldiers of the garrison. As if the citadel wasn't enough, the Grand or Royal Battery stood on the mainland to cover the harbor entrance with thirty cannon. The Island Battery with thirty-nine cannon was on an island just inside the harbor en-

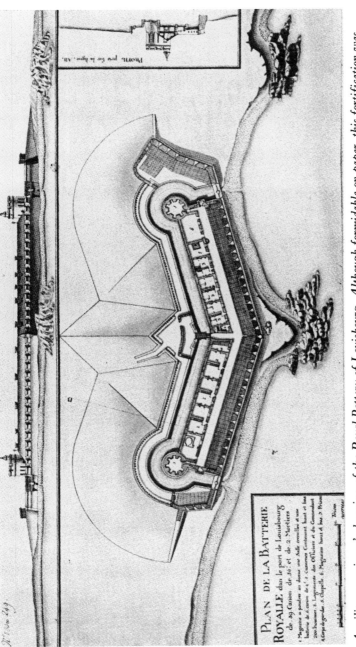

A military engineer's drawing of the Royal Battery of Louisbourg. Although formidable on paper, this fortification was abandoned without a struggle in two wars.

trance. No fleet could enter the harbor until these batteries were put out of action.

Cape Breton Island is one of the gloomiest places in North America. Nature seems to have given it only two seasons: early winter and late winter. The wind blows constantly from the north and northeast, off the ocean. Fogs lasting weeks turn everything soggy and gray; they are so thick that you can taste the salt in the air.

Louisbourg was hard duty for a soldier. The garrison lived in cramped barracks, sleeping two to a bunk on straw-filled sacks; the straw, changed only once a year, stank of sweat and feet, and crawled with bugs. When they weren't scratching, soldiers had nothing to do with their off-duty time but gamble, drink, and fight among themselves. Pay, *if* it came twice a year, wasn't enough to meet a man's needs. Morale was poor, and Louis de Chambon, governor of the citadel, wasn't sure how well his men would fight if the English came. He'd soon find out.

The long peace ended in March 1744. As usual, war traveled from east to west, beginning in Europe and spreading to North America. Known as the War of the Austrian Succession, it was fought to decide who would succeed to, or inherit, the throne of Austria. This time England's King George II gave his name to the struggle in the colonies.

Indian war parties resumed hit-and-run raids on frontier settlements. The Sieur de Marin, a French nobleman, led a band into New York to burn Saratoga and set ambushes from Albany to Schenectady. The Five Nations joined the struggle, attacking French settlements along the St. Lawrence. The savagery of these raids is revealed in a letter a young Frenchman named Beaujeu de Vilmonde wrote to his father on March 27, 1747:

I attacked a house where there were twenty-five English, all armed to the teeth. Rushing to the door, I came suddenly upon a sentry and killed him. I entered the house and they fired three or four

Defending her home. In this rough sketch from A Narrative of the Captivity, Sufferings, and Removes of Mrs. Mary Rowlandson *(Boston, 1791), the lady of the house fires on a group of Indians.*

shots at me, which only passed through my greatcoat. I fired my pistols at the captain, whom I killed; then I gave the sergeant a bayonet thrust in the stomach and ran my gun through his body. He fell, his intestines protruding from his stomach, and I withdrew my gun, which was broken. I snatched the gun from another Englishman who had caught me by the neck; happily, I was the stronger, and I killed him. I clubbed another one to death, and outside I fired on a fleeing Englishman and broke his arm.

The battle for Louisbourg became the main event in King George's War. The town might not have been attacked had it not been for the French themselves. News of the declaration of war reached Canada before the English colonies. Governor de Chambon decided to strike immediately, while the enemy was still off guard. In May 1744, he sent a force to capture Canseau, a fishing village in northern Acadia, across the narrow strait from Cape

Breton Island. Canseau's defenders, outnumbered and out-gunned, surrendered on condition that they be sent to Boston. Until travel arrangements could be made, they were taken to Louisbourg, where they kept their eyes open. They memorized the layout of the citadel, counted its guns, and listened to the garrison's complaints. No sooner did they reach Boston than they told everything to the governor.

Massachusetts Governor William Shirley was determined to take Louisbourg even if his colony did the job by itself. Soon Boston was buzzing with talk of his plan. Its supporters believed that, with a little Yankee luck, the fortress could be captured. Others strongly disagreed. No one in the colonies, they said, was experienced in siege warfare, let alone against such a modern fortress. Caution, they grumbled, was the best policy; let sleeping dogs lie. In Philadelphia, Benjamin Franklin adjusted his spectacles and took up his pen. "Fortified towns are hard nuts to crack," he warned his brother, John, in Boston, "and your teeth are not accustomed to it; but some seem to think that forts are as easy to take as snuff."

The Massachusetts Assembly ignored the warnings and voted money for a military expedition. Governor Shirley then sat down and wrote some letters of his own. The other New England colonies were invited to join Massachusetts in a crusade against Louisbourg.

For the first time, the colonies began to cooperate for a common purpose. Puritan preachers thundered from their pulpits, calling the faithful to arms. Recruiting parties accompanied by fifers and drummers tramped backwoods trails to enlist fighting men. Farm boys and college students, patriots and adventurers flocked to the colors.

William Pepperrell was chosen commander-in-chief with the rank of major general. Pepperrell, like Billy Phips, had never seen a moment's fighting in his life, let alone commanded an army. Yet as one of New England's leading merchants, he was a good organizer, skilled at getting people to work together. Above all, he was popular with the men, who, as volunteers, weren't used to military discipline. Independent-minded fellows, they'd sulk or desert if officers came down on them too hard.

During February and March 1745, a hundred ships assembled in Boston harbor from all over New England. Ninety were fishing boats to be used as troop-carriers. The remainder were armed sloops—small, swift craft mounting a few light cannon.

Boston became an armed camp. The recruiters had done well, signing up 4,270 fighting men. Massachusetts and Maine supplied 3,300, the largest group, followed by Connecticut's 516, and 454 from New Hampshire. Since there were no barracks, troops were "quartered", that is, private citizens fed them and gave them beds in their homes. It was the last bit of comfort many of them would ever enjoy.

Boston's waterfront became a vast open-air warehouse piled high with barrels, bundles, and bales of supplies, mostly food. Army food kept you alive, although no one, it seems, ever really liked it. The basic item was fatty pork preserved in barrels of brine; salt fish was packed dry and had to be softened with water before being eaten. Meat was eaten together with hardtack, an unleavened bread baked in slabs and hard as a dog biscuit. Dried peas and beans, rice, vinegar, butter, cheese, and sugar filled out the soldier's diet.

The most precious "food," however, came in small wooden kegs: rum. Make no mistake about it, rum was as necessary to the soldier's well-being as anything he ate. Its alcohol warmed his insides in the cold dampness of the camp, pepped him up on long marches, and dulled his aches and pains. Rum fortified his courage in battle and, if wounded, helped him face the surgeon's knife. No wonder he sang about rum as "God's great gift." No wonder, too, that many men left the army as alcoholics.

The most important fighting tools were the artillery. Each piece was worth its weight in gold, for without cannon the army

would smash itself like the ocean's waves against the walls of Louisbourg.

The Yankees had thirty cannon, mostly lightweights able to fire twenty-two-, eighteen-, and nine-pound iron balls half a mile. In addition, there were four mortars—short, stubby-barreled guns for lobbing explosive shells over hills and walls. Yet these were popguns, compared to the monsters protecting Louisbourg. The French guns weighed over three tons each and could hurl a forty-two-pound ball a mile.

Pepperrell wasn't worried. Somehow he had found a supply of forty-two-pounder balls, which he loaded aboard the fleet. And the guns to shoot them? Where would he get them? Why, from the French, of course. He expected to capture whatever he needed early in the battle and turn them against their former owners. That, said doubting Thomases, was "like selling the skin of a bear before catching him."

On March 24, 1745, the fleet sailed amid the cheers of well-wishers and the clanging of church bells. Shipboard life soon became a nightmare for the troops, most of whom had never been on an ocean-going vessel before. There were no bunks; each man had a hammock strung belowdecks or bedded down on the raw floorboards. Few had a full night's sleep. Rats scampered over the men's faces, pushing their pink snouts into their pockets in search of food. The air was heavy with the odor of candlewax and stale codfish.

To make matters worse, the fleet sailed into the teeth of a northeastern gale. The wind howled, lashing the vessels with sheets of rain. The flimsy craft heaved and shook, bounced and rolled, all at the same time. "This day," a soldier scrawled in his

William Pepperrell was a merchant who became a general and led the New Englanders in the assault on Louisbourg in 1745. From a painting in the Essex Institute, Salem, Massachusetts, by John Smibert.

diary, "our Vessel was A Very Hospital, wee were all Sick, in a Greater or Less Degree." Men lay on their backs, moaning and vomiting over themselves.

Even the seamen were miserable. One captain became too ill to manage his vessel. His first mate took over, but he "was Something Disguised with Liquor," that is, too drunk to see straight. An old fisherman had to do the steering, although he knew nothing about navigation. The troops belowdecks cursed the day they'd heard the name Louisbourg.

The fleet rode out the storm and anchored at Canseau two weeks later, easily retaking it from the tiny French garrison. There they spent most of April, repairing damage and waiting for the ice to break up in Louisbourg harbor.

In the meantime, they were joined by Commodore Peter Warren, commander of the Royal Navy's Caribbean squadron. Warren, who lived in New York City and owned a parcel of land called Greenwich Village, brought three men-of-war with a combined firepower of 140 big guns. With these, Warren could prevent enemy ships from coming to Louisbourg's rescue, allowing the ground forces to pound it to smithereens at their leisure.

On the last day of April 1745, lookouts at the Island Battery saw puffs of white on the horizon.

Soon, with drums beating and flags flying, Commodore Warren's squadron lined up broadside to the Island Battery and opened fire. Across the water, in Louisbourg, alarm bells sounded, calling the defenders to battle stations.

As Warren dueled with the Island Battery, Pepperrell led the transports to the landing site. The Canseau prisoners had told him everything he needed to know.

Three miles west of the town, at Gabarus Bay, a narrow finger of land known as Flat Point pointed seaward. A fine landing place, 75 Frenchmen were dug in above the beach, waiting. Two miles beyond was an inlet called Fresh Water Cove. This was undefended.

Sir Peter Warren, commander of the British squadron at Louisbourg, 1745.

The transports anchored off Flat Point and began to lower assault boats. When the boats were filled, sailors cast off and began to pull for shore. Slowly, like clumsy water beetles, the boats neared the waiting enemy. Nearer, nearer they came until a signal flag unfurled from the mast of Pepperrell's ship. Instantly the boats veered left and sped toward Fresh Water Cove. The French raced after them, but since the curve of the shore gave the French a longer route, the boats outpaced them.

The first wave leaped into the chest-high surf. Yelping at the shock of the icy water, the Yankees waded in with muskets and powder horns held over their heads. They landed in time to take cover behind boulders and drive off the breathless Frenchmen. By sundown, the army was ashore without losing a man.

That night, the Yankees sat around brushwood fires singing, joking, and gulping rum. Since there hadn't been time to unload the tents, they slept on the ground in wet clothes, lashed by the cold wind. Rum, at least, made the ordeal bearable.

Pepperell was eager to get down to business as soon as possible. At dawn, he sent a scouting party under Colonel William Vaughan into the hilly country north of the harbor. There, in the woods behind the Grand Battery, Vaughan found warehouses full of naval stores—tar, pitch, paint, rope, sails—which he burned. The wind carried clouds of greasy smoke over the Grand Battery, shrouding it completely for minutes at a time.

While patrolling next morning, Vaughan noticed something strange. The Grand Battery was silent. Nothing stirred inside. Its flagpole was empty. Suspecting a trick, he bribed a Cape Cod Indian with a bottle of brandy to sneak up to the fortress and have a look around. After a few swigs of "liquid courage," the brave crept up to a gun port and wriggled through the opening. Moments later he reappeared, waving his arms.

Vaughan had hit the jackpot. The Grand Battery was deserted, abandoned either because there weren't enough troops to man it or in panic after being enveloped in smoke the day before. Private William Tufts of Massachusetts shinnied up the flagstaff and tied his red coat at the top.

The French had made an awful mistake. Instead of blowing the Grand Battery sky-high, they'd left it in perfect condition; the underground ammunition rooms were full of barrels of gunpowder and shot. The only damage was to the guns, which had been "spiked." A steel spike was hammered into the touchhole at the rear of each cannon, preventing it from being fired. But they had been spiked so poorly that Yankee gunsmiths easily repaired the weapons. Pepperrell's idea of bringing along forty-two-pound shot hadn't been so harebrained after all.

Losing the Grand Battery weakened, but didn't cripple, Louisbourg's defenses. To do that, the Yankees had to place their own cannon around the citadel. This was easier said than done, for the bulky weapons had to be rowed ashore in flat-bottomed barges. It was exhausting, dangerous work to manage these clumsy craft in the surging waves and undertows. Most barges were smashed to splinters against the rocks.

Yet the Yankee sailors wouldn't give up. It became a matter of pride with them to see the guns safely to the beach. And they paid the price. Every gun landed meant strained muscles, crushed fingers, and broken limbs. At last, the bulky weapons—all of them —stood on the hard-packed sand at the water's edge.

Now came the really difficult task. The guns had to be moved from the beach to a range of low hills behind the citadel, a distance of three miles. Since there were no oxen and few horses, men had to attach anchor cables to the guns and heave away with their bare hands. Two hundred men were needed to drag each gun over the soft beach sand and the rocks beyond. The last obstacle was a half-mile strip of marsh that lay between some woods and the hills. The first men to step into the marsh sank up to their chests in the slippery slime. Wheeled gun carriages stuck fast in the mud, and no amount of heaving or cursing could budge them. All the while, Louisbourg's cannon rained death on the struggling Yankees.

Colonel Nathaniel Meserve of New Hampshire came to the rescue. "Stone boats," he advised, "build stone boats." New Englanders cleared their fields for planting by heaping stones on sledges, or boats, drawn by oxen. Meserve wanted to build giant sledges, sixteen feet long by five wide, that would actually *float* over the marsh.

His idea worked. Under cover of darkness, hundreds of men harnessed themselves to the stone boats and began to pull. It was like bathing in cold, brown, smelly glue. The mud sucked the shoes off their feet; then it took their stockings. Barefoot, they slid and fell into the muck.

"Praise God from Whom all blessings flow," a soldier sang. Soon everyone was pulling on the ropes in time to the music. Even officers lent a hand. Pepperrell waded into the ooze, still wearing his general's coat of scarlet and gold. Soldiers shouted themselves hoarse and slipped and pulled. The guns moved.

Four days later, Governor de Chambon stared speechless from the citadel wall. There, on the hills to the east, stood Yankee guns, polished and menacing. A puff of smoke. A booming echo. Seconds later an iron ball slammed into the fortress. He could already see the end of Louisbourg.

Until then, few New Englanders had ever fired a cannon. Gunpowder was expensive and not to be wasted in target practice. Gunnery training consisted of endless dry runs to build up speed in loading; a fast crew could fire a forty-two-pounder thirty times a day.

Cannon were loaded from the muzzle. First, the correct amount of gunpowder was shoveled into the barrel. A ball was then rolled down, followed by a wad of old ropes, and everything packed tight with a rammer, a pole tipped with a large wooden knob. Firing was done by touching a burning rope to some fine-grained gunpowder in the touchhole, a cuplike indentation cut into the top of the barrel. The powder flashed, sending a jet of flame downward to explode the main charge inside the gun. After each shot, a damp sheepskin was used to clean the barrel; this prevented particles of smoldering gunpowder from igniting the next charge in the crew's faces.

The New Englanders had much to learn about gunnery. Excited men experiencing battle for the first time double-loaded their cannon. The resulting explosions burst the barrels, hurling chunks of hot iron through the air. Heads were torn off shoulders; arms and legs seemed to rain from the sky. Men fifty feet away were flattened to a bloody pulp.

The Yankees learned gunnery slowly, painfully, but they learned well. By the end of the first week, they'd found Louisbourg's range and began a steady bombardment from the hilltops and the Grand Battery.

The bombardment was awesome, like the forces of nature unleashed. Mortar shells arched skyward, paused for an instant at the top of their arc, and fell screaming to earth. Cannonballs slammed into the outer wall, into the citadel and into the town itself. Streets were plowed from end to end. Houses shuddered for a moment, then flew apart in a shower of splinters and masonry. A cloud of dust hung over the place, pointing to the destruction beneath.

The defenders struck back as best they could. Sharpshooters picked off Yankee gunners, only to see others rush forward to take their places. French cannon bellowed in retaliation.

Doctors on both sides were busy with the wounded. Hospitals in the 1700s weren't anything like our own today. Any building—house, barn, stable, church, privy—might serve as a hospital. "The wounded," wrote a New Englander, "lay ranged in double rows on piles of loose straw. Some moaned steadily; others, to stifle their agony, chewed leather straps or blocks of soft pine."

There were no painkillers. Before surgery, the patient was given as much rum as he could swallow. When the rum took effect, and his head reeled, the doctor's helpers made him "bite the bullet," that is, they put a musket ball between his teeth to keep him from biting off his tongue during the operation. While the helpers held him down, the doctor probed for the bullet with a long steel instrument, or sawed off a limb. Many wounded men died of pain, shock, and loss of blood.

Even a scratch could kill. There were no antibiotics, then, and no knowledge that dirt caused infection. Wounds weren't washed; doctors washed their hands *after* an operation, not before. If a scalpel fell to the ground, the doctor snatched it up, wiped it on his bloodstained apron, and continued cutting. No wonder soldiers were more frightened of getting wounded than of being killed outright.

The Island Battery, meanwhile, kept Warren's ships from entering the harbor to give close-in fire support. It had to be taken.

Toward midnight, May 26, 1745, 400 men crowded into assault boats and shoved off from the beach beneath the Grand Battery. The night was inky black, the sea calm, and they used paddles instead of oars to keep the noise down. Within the hour, the boats were bobbing gently in the swells outside a tiny cove. No sentries were posted, and the swivel guns on the seawall were unmanned. No one in the Island Battery expected an attack that night.

The raiders landed and were advancing when a drunken soldier began to cheer. Several comrades, who'd also filled up on liquid courage, gave three loud cheers in return.

Those drunkards turned easy victory into bitter defeat. The French, alerted, answered their cheers with gunfire. Tongues of orange flame cut the darkness. Men screamed. The raiders stampeded for the boats, each man thinking only of his own safety. They crowded into the boats, dying like fish shot in a barrel.

Daylight brought an end to the unequal fight. One hundred nineteen Yankees who had been left behind surrendered. Seventy bodies were counted. Nearly half the landing force had been lost. It was now the Frenchmen's turn to cheer, albeit not for long.

Pepperrell wasn't a good loser. Defeat only made him more stubborn, more determined to have his way, whatever the cost. He ordered cannon hauled to Lighthouse Point across from the Island Battery to pound the battery day and night. Gradually, its guns were knocked off their mountings and its walls began to come apart at the seams. On June 15, a mortar shell broke through the roof of the main ammunition room and exploded with an earsplitting *bar-ooom*. That afternoon, drummer boys mounted the citadel wall and rapped out the signal for a truce. De Chambon wanted to discuss surrender terms.

Pepperrell was prepared to be generous. If the French surrendered, he promised to protect the lives and property of Louisbourg's citizens. Its garrison would enjoy the "honors of war," that is, the troops could march out with flags flying, drums beating, and bayonets fixed. But if the enemy held out against all odds, forcing Pepperrell to take Louisbourg by infantry assault, citizens and garrison would probably be wiped out by the angry Yankees.

The French decided to keep their honor and their lives. The victors, however, had nothing to show for their efforts beyond their pay of sixpence (six cents) a day. Many were poor countryfolk who had to struggle for a living. Dreams of taking Louisbourg's wealth had inspired hundreds to join the expedition. They expected to loot the town; indeed, it was their *right* to loot it. Looting captured towns was normal in the 1700s, a way of paying the troops at the enemy's expense.

But Pepperrell had promised that there would be no looting. The troops felt wronged, betrayed, and let him know it with shouted insults. "A great Noys and hubbub a mongst ye Soldiers a bout ye Plunder," one wrote in his diary. "Som a Cursing, Som a Swarein."

The seamen, however, did better. No sooner had the French flag been lowered than Warren had it raised again. He was setting out honey to catch flies. Sure enough, some French ships saw the flag and, not knowing that the town had fallen, sailed into the

The French decided to accept William Pepperrell's generous offer to protect the people of Louisbourg if they surrendered rather than continue the battle to the end.

harbor, right under the guns of Warren's squadron. The ships' cargoes, worth ten million dollars in today's money, were later sold and the profits distributed among the English sailors as "prize" money. The soldiers received nothing.

News of the victory reached Boston two weeks later. Clanging church bells and booming cannons awakened the city in the

middle of the night. Before sunup, shouting, singing crowds filled the narrow streets. The wave of happiness rolled out from Boston to Philadelphia, New York, and Newport, Rhode Island, where tubs of rum-punch were set up in the streets for all to enjoy. Across the sea, the great guns in the Tower of London boomed in triumph.

Yet Louisbourg, like any victory, hadn't come without cost. French losses were light—120 killed and wounded. Yankee casualties were 330. Unfortunately, the worst was still to come. Until they could be relieved by British troops, Pepperrell's army had to occupy the ruined town. During the winter of 1745–1746, a thousand Yankees died of cold and disease.

And they died for nothing. When the Treaty of Aix-la-Chapelle ended the war in 1748, King George II returned Louisbourg to France in exchange for territory in India. It was a slap in the face to New England. By ignoring the colonists' sacrifices, the British government showed that it thought only of the interests of the mother country. From then on, the spark of an idea began to glow in colonists' minds: Perhaps they would be better off on their own. But as long as New France threatened them, they needed England's protection. Once that threat was removed, the spark would burst into flame twenty-eight years later, in 1776.

❧❧❧III❦❦❦

George Washington Sets the World on Fire

G EORGE WASHINGTON at twenty-one was a mature man ready to take a man's part in the world. Broad-shouldered, with long, muscular arms and legs, he stood over six feet tall in his moccasins. He had a straight nose, blue eyes, a face pitted with smallpox scars, and a large mouth that was usually kept shut, perhaps from embarrassment at his poor teeth; he'd lose them all in time, replacing them with dentures of ivory and wood.

Years as a land surveyor in backwoods Virginia had hardened his body and given him self-confidence. Calm, patient, and serious, young Washington, folks agreed, was a born leader. Already a major in the militia, one day he'd lead armies.

Now, in the autumn of 1753, he set out on a mission that would trigger the last, and bloodiest, of the French and Indian Wars.

WASHINGTON'S MISSION was the idea of Virginia Governor Robert Dinwiddie. The governor had been spending sleepless nights lately, for he had learned that the French were up to no good in the West, in the valley of the Ohio River. Ever since the end of King George's War, English and French traders and frontiersmen had become interested in the lands watered by the Ohio. The French called it *La Belle Rivière*—"the Beautiful River"—and they were right. The river and the country it flowed through reminded travelers of the biblical Garden of Eden. Prairies, forests, and lakes stretched unbroken for thousands of square miles. Buffalo and deer roamed in vast herds, munching the lush grass and enriching the soil with their droppings. The waterways swarmed with fish and were covered with brightly colored ducks and geese. The graceful passenger pigeon, now extinct, blotted out the sun in flights of tens of millions; Indians had only to lift a net to snare a dozen birds at a time. The land was said to be so fertile that any plant grew to at least twice its usual size there.

Both the English and French wanted to control the Ohio country. The English were eager to cut into the French fur trade and open new lands to settlement. The French were more ambitious; they saw an opportunity to win all the land from the Ohio to the Rockies and beyond.

A glance at the map will show what they had in mind. Rivers were the keys to unlocking the treasures of North America. America in the 1750s had no roads other than Indian trails through the forests. Narrow, rugged, and often blocked by fallen trees, they made it impossible to move heavy cargo long distances; people traveled at a snail's pace. For example, eight days was needed to go from Boston to New York *in good weather*, another

The young George Washington wearing his uniform of the French and Indian War. Notice the gorget, the crescent-shaped badge worn around the neck indicating that he is an officer. This portrait by Charles Willson Peale is the only one done of him before the American Revolution, in 1772, and belongs to Washington and Lee University.

three days to go from New York to Philadelphia. Whenever you traveled, you tried to go by water.

America is blessed by a marvelous system of waterways. European rivers all flow away from one another. Our rivers, however, interlock, tying together the farthest corners of the land. And our most important rivers are the Ohio and Mississippi, forming a vast system that drains the continent between Lake Erie and the Gulf of Mexico, the Appalachian Mountains and the Rockies.

French control of this river system would allow them to do two things. First, they could link Canada with their Louisiana territory and the city of New Orleans at the mouth of the Mississippi. More important, they could isolate the English colonies. Blocked from the interior by the Appalachian Mountains, the colonies would be pinned forever to a narrow strip along the Atlantic coast. Governor Dinwiddie had good reason to be concerned.

Both sides claimed the Ohio country. Virginians said that it was part of their western frontier, granted by royal charter to the Jamestown settlers. Canadians disagreed, claiming it as a result of the Sieur de la Salle's explorations in the 1670s. Sooner or later the question of ownership would have to be settled by force. And the French were determined to land the first blow.

Virginia and Pennsylvania fur traders had built a few log cabins at Pickawillany (Piqua, Ohio). Local Indians were so friendly to them that their chief became known as Old Britain. In June 1753, the Marquis de Duquesne, governor of New France, sent a war party of Ottawa and Chippewa to teach them a lesson. He meant it to be a harsh lesson, one not easily forgotten. The trading post was destroyed and the traders killed. Old Britain was butchered, boiled, and eaten by the braves.

Duquesne next began to seal off the river-roads to the West. He ordered Fort Presque Isle built on the southern shore of Lake Erie and then had a road cut ten miles to the head of French

Creek. Fort Le Boeuf was built to guard this site. Fort Venango rose a few miles downstream, where French Creek joins the Allegheny River. It was here on a cold, drizzly day before Christmas 1753, that George Washington rode out of the woods with six companions.

Governor Dinwiddie had sent him on a spying mission under cover of delivering a message to the French. He was to pinpoint the French strongholds and find out how many men were in each. He must also draw accurate maps of the area, noting likely sites for new forts.

Washington, his surveyor's notebook in hand, made a most careful description of one spot, "the Forks of the Ohio." He stood on a rocky wedge of land observing the scene around him. From his right flowed the Allegheny, highway to the French forts, Lake Erie, and Canada. From his left flowed the Monongahela, reaching back toward the Potomac Valley. They joined at his feet to form the Beautiful River, the mighty Ohio. This was the most valuable piece of property in America in 1753. For whoever controlled it, he knew, controlled also the gateway to the West.

Washington and his party rode up to Fort Le Boeuf, where he delivered Dinwiddie's message to the local French commander. The message was a demand that the intruders leave His Majesty's territory immediately.

The commander, one-eyed Captain Legardeur de St. Pierre, was in no mood to hear demands. Politely, but firmly, he insisted that the Ohio country belonged to France and that Englishmen had better stay out. His orders were to capture any trespassers, and he intended to obey them to the letter. There was nothing else to discuss.

Washington's return trip was as painful as any captives' march. The temperature plummeted, and freezing rain shrouded the trees in ice. No time to waste now! Winter was coming, and they had to move quickly or be trapped in the wilderness at the mercy of the French. But animals and men were reaching the limits of their strength. The horses went lame, so Washington had to leave them with the men while he went forward on foot with Christopher Gist, an experienced frontiersman.

It was rough going. Near an Indian village called Murthering Town, a brave shot at them, narrowly missing Washington before escaping into the forest. On the bank of the Allegheny, they built a raft to carry them downstream. The rushing river was full of ice blocks, which overturned the raft. The two men swam to an island, where they spent the night without a fire, encased in an envelope of ice. After other hardships and narrow escapes, they reached Williamsburg, the Virginia capital, early in January 1754.

Governor Dinwiddie now had all the information he needed. In the spring, he sent Ensign Edward Ward and 40 woodsmen to build a fort at the Forks of the Ohio. Washington, soon to be promoted to colonel, was to follow in a few weeks with a military force to defend the fort. His orders were short and crisp. He was not to look for trouble, but if anyone tried to interfere, " . . . you are to restrain all such offenders and, in case of resistance, to make prisoners of or to kill and destroy them."

Washington moved slowly. Once he had left Virginia's western settlements, he had to lead his men over the Alleghenies, the southern portion of the great Appalachian range. Climbing the mountains was difficult enough for men on foot or horseback; it was a nightmare for a force with a wagon train. The mountains and the valleys beyond were covered with giant trees knitted together with tangled vines. Axmen had to go ahead, hacking out a trail every inch of the way. Most days, the column was lucky to go two miles before halting, exhausted, for the night.

Washington's impatience turned to anger when scouts reported that the French had surprised Ensign Ward, wrecked his half-completed fort, and were building a much larger fort of their own—Fort Duquesne.

Frontier forts were of two types. The type favored by settlers was a simple wooden stockade built around a settlement. Axmen began by cutting heavy posts or pickets from the forest, each at least a foot in diameter and twelve to fifteen feet in length. A rectangular ditch was then dug five feet into the ground and the pickets stood upright, one next to the other, forming a wall. Earth was shoveled into the ditch to keep the pickets in place and their tops sharpened to prevent attackers from climbing over. Gates were hung, loopholes cut every few feet, and a firing platform of half-split logs built at the proper height. Stockaded forts with plenty of water and food could hold out against Indians for months.

A military post like Fort Duquesne provided "defense in depth," meaning that the enemy had to break through several defense lines before penetrating the fort's heart. Designed by engineers, this type of fort was a smaller version of Louisbourg's citadel, only built of wood and earth instead of stone. Two walls of logs set horizontally were built twelve feet apart and the space between filled with tightly packed earth to form a single wall. This type of wall, called a "curtain," could withstand any weapon except heavy cannon. Bastions or strongpoints projected from each of the fort's four corners to catch attackers in a crossfire.

Inside the fort, cannon were mounted on platforms in the bastions and sometimes on the curtain walls themselves. The fort's buildings—barracks, officers' quarters, kitchen, bakery, storerooms, blacksmith's shop, prison—were clustered around an open area, or "parade," at the center. For good measure, the fort was surrounded by a wide, deep ditch, which was in turn surrounded by a stockade.

Washington, meanwhile, finally arrived at Great Meadows, a large clearing south of Fort Duquesne. He had just made camp when Chief Half-King of the Mingo, an Iroquoian-speaking tribe friendly to the English, found footprints. About 30 Frenchmen had a hidden camp in a gully only six miles away. Washington didn't know their mission, but had a pretty good idea. He remembered Captain St. Pierre's warning. He also knew his orders by heart. If the Frenchmen's intentions were peaceful, they would have come to him in the open, as he had at Fort Le Boeuf. By hiding, they must be preparing an ambush or waiting to guide a larger force to his camp. He decided to strike first.

Before dawn, May 28, 1754, Washington and his men crept through the wet woods, surrounding the French camp. Some of the soldiers were cooking breakfast, others still sleeping when he gave the signal.

The pop of muskets mingled with the Mingo war cry. Ten Frenchmen, including their leader, Captain Coulon de Jumonville, fell dead or dying. As Jumonville crumpled to the ground, Half-King cleaved his skull with a tomahawk and tore off his scalp. The survivors, 22 men, fought as best they could, but surrendered when they saw that resistance was useless.

Washington had fought his first battle, and he liked it. He wrote to his brother, Jack: "I heard the bullets whistle, and, believe me, there is something charming in the sound." Little did he know that that "charming" sound was the beginning of his problems. For young George Washington had started a war.

Several days later, a half-naked man stumbled through the gate of Fort Duquesne. Wild-eyed, with trembling voice he told the commander, Captain Claude-Pierre de Contrecoeur, how he'd escaped the ambush. Contrecoeur, a tough, old forest fighter, sprang into action. Messengers were sent racing through the Ohio country and into Canada. Wherever they went, birchbark canoes slid into the water. Militia, *coureurs de bois,* and braves converged on Fort Duquesne from every point of the compass.

By the end of June, fourteen hundred men were crowded into the fort and camped in the surrounding woods. Among them was Jumonville's elder brother, Captain Coulon de Villiers. Canadians called him "the Great Villiers," because he was fearless and never lost a fight. Contrecoeur gave him nine hundred men and sent him to punish his brother's "assassins."

After destroying Jumonville's party, Washington returned to Great Meadows. From now on, he was racing the clock. The French, he knew, would soon come for their revenge and he had to be prepared. He put his four hundred men to work felling trees for a fort, which they named Fort Necessity.

Fort Necessity's only resemblance to a real fort was in its name. It was little more than a small, round stockade surrounded by shallow trenches. Worse, it was built in a natural bowl commanded by wooded hillsides, perfect cover for attackers. It was scarcely completed when Half-King and his braves vanished; they weren't going to throw away their lives in such a place.

When the French arrived, they found the Virginians waiting for them in battle formation. Washington had drawn them up in front of the trenches, hoping for a quick battle in the open; it was a gamble, he knew, but time was on the enemy's side and Fort Necessity could never withstand a siege.

Villiers, however, didn't take the bait. Instead of charging, he ordered his men to take cover, forcing the defenders behind the stockade and into the trenches. A thunderstorm burst, filling the trenches waist-deep with muddy water. Cold, hungry, and miserable, the Virginians battled their invisible enemy. All they could see were puffs of gunsmoke drifting upward from behind every rise in the ground, every tree, stump, and bush.

The French fire was murderous. Aiming carefully, they dropped anything that moved. Horses were deliberately shot; they even picked off the camp dogs. The muddy water in the trenches became streaked with human blood. Half the defenders were out of action by nightfall—sick, wounded, dead. Many who could still shoulder a musket were in no condition to fight. They'd broken into the rum stores to keep up their spirits and had became roaring drunk. The only thing to do was to ask for surrender terms.

Villiers was generous, probably because he believed enemy reinforcements were on the way. Next morning, after freeing his prisoners, Washington marched away with the honors of war. It was a sad, heartbreaking march, the first of many in his career. Nor would he ever forget the date: the Fourth of July.

The shots fired in that forest clearing echoed across the ocean and across the world. The struggle for the Ohio country was becoming serious, and since the stakes were so high, neither side could afford to back down. Although the mother countries were still at peace, they began preparing for war. Orders went out from London and Paris to outfit warships and bring regiments up to strength for service in America. The regulars were coming at last.

Regulars were very different from colonial militiamen. Militiamen were part-time soldiers who went home when their enlistments expired after a few weeks or months. Regulars were career soldiers, members of a nation's standing army.

The armies of old Europe were officered by gentlemen and the ranks filled by the unemployed, the adventurous, even the criminal; convicts were often allowed to choose between jail or the army. When a man enlisted, he expected to serve until he became too old or too crippled for active duty. The army, in fact, became his home and family. If he married, his wife shared his bed in the barracks; married families had no privacy. A certain number of soldiers' wives always accompanied each regiment as "necessary women" to cook, wash, and tend the wounded. Army wives marched behind their men, sharing the hardships and dangers of the campaign.

The soldier was not taught to think for himself or to act on his own. He was actually a uniformed machine trained to advance in closed ranks to within a few yards of an enemy column. Then, on command, each side fired its muskets at point-blank range.

Volley after volley was exchanged, enveloping the battlefield in the "fog of battle," dense clouds of gray gunsmoke. If one side seemed to be gaining the upper hand, it charged to victory with the bayonet. Casualties in this style of warfare were usually very high.

Men do not naturally face death, or step over the mangled bodies of friends, without flinching. To get them to do so, they were drilled until their actions became automatic. Discipline was harsh and brutal. The least wavering, the slightest disobedience, brought punishment no Indian brave would tolerate. A soldier could be whipped hundreds of times on the bare back for a minor offense; if he fainted during the ordeal, a bucket of saltwater on the open wounds revived him. English regulars were called "red-coats" and "bloodybacks," owing to the color of their uniform and harsh discipline.

The uniform was itself an aid to discipline. Skintight, with a peaked brass helmet, it forced the soldier to stand erect. The red coat, too, served a purpose. It was *meant* to be seen in order to prevent friendly troops from firing at each other in the fog of battle. Red also concealed bloodstains, useful in preventing panic when someone was hit in the closely packed ranks; warship decks were painted red for the same reason. French regulars' uniforms were white, which easily distinguished them from the enemy in battle.

The British regulars in North America were commanded by Major General Edward Braddock. Short, fat, and red faced, Braddock at sixty was known as a soldier's soldier. He had been in the army since the age of fifteen and had a reputation for raw courage, iron discipline, and bad temper. During the War of the Spanish Succession, he had seen plenty of fighting in the Low Countries and Germany. If anyone could save the Ohio country, it was this veteran.

Braddock landed in Virginia in February 1755, with two

regiments, the Forty-fourth and Forty-eighth Foot. This was the largest force of British infantrymen ever sent to the colonies, and he intended to use them wisely.

Upon arriving, he called the colonial governors to a conference at Alexandria, Virginia, to explain his plans. His strategy called for attacking the French at three key points. Braddock would lead the regulars in person against Fort Duquesne. Massachusetts Governor Shirley was to capture Fort Niagara between Lake Erie and Lake Ontario with colonial militia, cutting Canada's east-west water route. William Johnson, Commissioner of Indian Affairs, would lead an expedition against Crown Point near the southern end of Lake Champlain. At the same time, a New England force would deal with the French settlers in Acadia.

Braddock soon found that it was easier to make plans than to carry them out. Although the colonial assemblies welcomed his redcoats, they refused to contribute to a common defense fund. Since colonies belonged to their mother country, they insisted that all defense costs be paid by the English taxpayer.

As a result of their stinginess, Braddock's army was tormented by supply problems. Food often arrived late and was of poor quality; spoiled meat stank so badly that it had to be buried the moment a barrel was opened. There were never enough wagons—not for the troops to ride in, but to haul food, supplies, and fodder.

The general came to hate Americans. They were cowardly weaklings, he shouted, his face flushed, the veins bulging in his neck. To all who saw his temper, he seemed more inclined to fight the colonists than to defend them.

Only two Americans were the equals of Englishmen in Braddock's eyes. George Washington, whom he invited to be his aide, served as an unpaid volunteer. He was always considerate of the younger man, always spoke kindly to him, and asked his advice. A real friendship grew up between the two men. Braddock was also proud to call Benjamin Franklin his friend. As postmaster general of the colonies, Franklin found enough horses and wagons for the march inland.

Franklin was equally generous with advice and warned against the dangers of ambush. Braddock only laughed at his concern. His regiments, he said, could easily handle anything the French might send against them. As for the "savages," their Indian allies, he considered them merely two-legged animals. They might worry the militia, "but upon the king's regular and disciplined troops, sir, it is impossible they should make an impression." He expected a hard trek over the Alleghenies, but he assured Franklin that he would need only four days to take Fort Duquesne.

Braddock's army began to assemble at Fort Cumberland, Virginia, in April 1755. In addition to fourteen hundred redcoats, he had thirty sailors and five hundred "blues," blue-uniformed colonials from Virginia, Maryland, and the Carolinas—in all some two thousand men. There were also several hundred axmen, wagon drivers, and necessary women.

The army was built around its power-hitters, the cannon. Without these, it hadn't a prayer of denting the fort's defenses. Cannon would punch holes in its earth-and-wood walls, forcing the garrison to surrender or fight to the death. As in European sieges, there was a good chance that the French would surrender after the first few breaches appeared in the walls and honor had been satisfied. Braddock's artillery train included four twelve-pounder "ship killers" borrowed from the navy, plus twelve six-pounders and nineteen other guns, mostly small mortars.

On June 10, 1755, the gates of Fort Cumberland swung open. Braddock, on horseback, gave the order and drummers began to rap out the marching signal. Sergeants bawled commands. Wagon drivers cracked their whips. Within a few hours, a column four miles long was moving behind a cloud of dust toward the western mountains.

On the march. Dense columns of Braddock's army march through the wilderness on their way to defeat by the French near Fort Duquesne.

Washington's expedition had been a picnic, compared with the march of the regulars. Although they followed the trail he'd opened, axmen had to widen every inch of it for the wagon train and artillery. Still, "Braddock's Road" was merely a tunnel, darkened by overhanging branches, plunging through the forest. An officer complained that it was impossible to see more than twenty feet ahead or to the right and left.

Heat and fatigue began to sap the army's strength. Almost at once, the route pitched upward toward the Alleghenies. Wagons tipped over, shattering against boulders. Horses dropped dead on the steep grades. Sailors, handy with block and tackle, strained to get the guns across the deep ravines. Teamsters shouted foul curses and drove their teams forward. Among them was a North Carolina lad who'd sit around campfires at night listening to tales of a glorious land beyond the mountains. Then and there Daniel Boone vowed that one day he'd settle in Kentucky.

The redcoats suffered the most. These soldiers, used to campaigns in the lowlands of Belgium and along the Rhine, had never seen such rugged country. Every step brought its own special type of pain and fear. Swarms of gnats buzzed around their heads, getting into their eyes, nostrils, and mouths. Chiggers with bites like hot sparks burrowed under the skin. Snakes with rattles in their tails made them speechless with fear. And beyond each ridge stretched other mountains and forests with such names as Savage Mountain and Shades of Death.

The Americans took pleasure in telling horror stories about their land. The Indians were crueler than demons, they said. No beastliness—scalping, torture, cannibalism—was beyond them. The stories began to have an effect. At night, huddled around watch fires, redcoats cried out in their sleep. The army's morale, its fighting spirit and will to win, began to crack long before it crossed the Alleghenies.

These horror stories softened up the redcoats for what came next. French and Indian patrols had been shadowing them since Fort Cumberland. As the redcoats advanced, the Indians tacked fresh scalps to trees along the trail. Stragglers were butchered and chunks of their flesh left for the redcoats to see. They understood these messages as clearly as any written warning. "Go away!" they warned. "Go back where you belong or you'll be next!"

Despite heroic efforts, the army moved at a snail's pace. Most days it was lucky to make three miles between dawn and dusk. At this rate, supplies would run out before reaching the Ohio country.

On June 19, Braddock called his officers together to discuss the problem. George Washington arrived with a splitting headache and ringing ears. Although he didn't know it then, he had typhoid fever and would be flat on his back for the next two weeks. His mind, however, was clear enough to suggest the best plan of action. The army must be split into two divisions. The first division, led by Braddock, should be a streamlined striking force of fourteen hundred of the best men. Armed with a few light cannon, its food and equipment slung on packhorses, it could dash to the Ohio. The second division would follow at its own pace with the wagons and heavy guns.

Washington wasn't with his general when Braddock left the next morning. He lay burning with fever in a cart that bumped along with the second division. He stayed in that cart until it arrived at Great Meadows. As a doctor helped him down, he saw the ruins of Fort Necessity overgrown with weeds. Although weak and dizzy, he left to rejoin Braddock the next morning, exactly a year after his defeat. He was glad to leave that place and its memories behind.

Washington caught up with Braddock at a bend in the Monongahela ten miles below Fort Duquesne. He noticed right away that the army's mood had improved since he'd seen it last. The men were cheerful, joking and laughing for the first time since leaving the Virginia settlements. Warnings were still found tacked to trees, but the enemy never showed himself. Everybody from Braddock on down wondered if the French meant to fight or were bluffing. A rumor spread through the camp that Fort Duquesne had been abandoned. All that the redcoats would have to do was to march in and enjoy the Frenchman's brandy before moving on to Canada. Washington was also happy, even though he had to keep a pillow on his saddle to ease the pain of riding. He'd arrived just in time to have his revenge for Fort Necessity.

All was well. No enemy in sight. Henry Gordon, a Royal Engineer, recalled how his comrades "hugged themselves with joy at their good luck." Victory was in the air; they could taste it, feel it in their bones.

Braddock turned the river crossing into a parade. The main body swung down the bank into the water, with flags flying and drums beating. A band stood on a hillock with fifes shrilling "The Grenadiers' March." The sun glinted on polished gun barrels, bayonets, and brass helmets. Reflections of scarlet and blue shimmered in the rippling water. Here, Washington thought, was war in all its color and pageantry. He'd recall years later, as president of the United States, that this had been the most thrilling sight of his life.

The army advanced cautiously, each unit in its proper place, doing its own task. A spearhead of scouts and Virginia cavalry led the way into the forest. Behind them came an advance guard of three hundred under Lieutenant Colonel Thomas Gage; twenty years later, *General* Gage would send redcoats to seize military supplies at Concord, Massachusetts, triggering the American Revolution. Gage's men screened a hundred axmen, who cleared and widened the trail for the main body—eight hundred men under Braddock. This was followed by the light cannon, ammunition wagons, and a company of necessary women. The rear guard came last. Flankers filtered through the woods on either side of the column to flush out snipers. There was no chance of being ambushed, as Benjamin Franklin had feared.

In the meantime, Captain Contrecoeur was making his own preparations. Indians had been bringing him reports of the enemy's movements for several weeks. He sensed that the tribesmen, true to their custom of avoiding pitched battles, might desert him at any moment.

Contrecoeur had only three hundred Frenchmen—regulars, Canadian militia, *coureurs de bois*—under his command. The neighboring woods concealed eight hundred braves. Some were Christian Caughnawaga, Abnaki, and Huron. The majority, however, were heathen Shawnee, Potawatomi, and Chippewa.

An Ottawa band was led by a princely looking chief with piercing eyes named Pontiac. There wasn't a hope of saving his fort without their help.

Contrecoeur knew that he had to defeat Braddock before the English arrived with their cannon. After discussing things with his officers, he decided to ambush the redcoats as they were crossing the Monongahela. He chose Captain Daniel Hyacinthe de Beaujeu to spring the trap.

The Indians loved Beaujeu as one of themselves. In the past, they had followed him on countless raids for English scalps and captives. Yet this time they held back. None would touch the red hatchet and black wampum he sent among them. "No, Father," they said, "you want to die and sacrifice yourself. The English are more than two thousand, and we are only eight hundred, and you want to go and attack them. We see clearly that you have no sense."

Next morning, July 9, Beaujeu mustered 150 Frenchmen to repel the invaders. Many were painted like Indians and naked except for breechcloths and moccasins. Beaujeu was among them; only the silver gorget, the half-moon-shaped officer's insignia worn around the neck, set him apart as their leader.

The Indians still refused to fight. "We cannot march," said a chief.

"What!" Beaujeu roared. "Will you let your father go alone?"

His reply, part question and part insult, hurt the warriors' pride. Instantly, three hundred gave the war whoop and demanded arms and ammunition. Barrels of gunpowder and musket balls were rolled out and broken open. Braves reached in, filling their powder horns and bullet pouches. A musket was issued to anyone who wanted one.

About eight hundred men dashed out of the fort and took the trail down to the Monongahela. They probably would have halted in their tracks had they known that Braddock's army was crossing at that very moment. There'd be no ambush today.

Colonel Gage's advance guard was moving nicely when the pointmen suddenly turned and fell back. Seconds later, Gage saw a painted "Indian" wearing a gorget. This Indian came running, waving a wide-brimmed hat, and the woods on either side of the trail swarmed with dark shapes.

"*Attaquez!*" he shouted. Attack!

The redcoats halted, closed ranks, and waited for orders. They were calm, their discipline perfect.

"Steady!" sergeants cried.

"Present!"

"Fire!"

Three hundred muskets went off with a single deafening *crack*. The attackers wavered, dazed by the volley, which did more harm to treetrunks than to men.

"*Attaquez! Attaquez!*" Beaujeu shouted again and again. He was so intent upon driving his men forward that he ignored the flaming muskets only yards away.

At the third volley, a hail of bullets destroyed his head. His followers, seeing him flop to the ground, cried, "*Sauve qui peut!* —"Every man for himself!" They were giving way without having fired a single shot.

"God save the king!" the redcoats cheered, and advanced with fixed bayonets, eager to finish off the enemy.

Only one man stepped forward to meet the glinting steel. Captain Dumas, Beaujeu's second-in-command, was a good soldier, but not a daring one. He surprised himself today. Without thinking, he stood in the open, shouting at the top of his voice: "Follow me! Fire! Kill them!"

Dumas's words and example stopped the panic. The tide of battle turned in favor of the French. Frenchmen turned around and began to shoot at the advancing redcoats. Indians dashed into the woods on either side of the path and began to fire at the redcoats' flanks. So began the greatest slaughter of British troops in the history of the New World.

Gage's men found themselves standing in the open in a U-shaped pocket with enemies firing from cover. Musket balls slashed through their ranks, breaking bones and killing men. Officers, towering above them on horseback, made easy targets. Within minutes, most of Gage's officers were riddled with lead. The men, almost leaderless, broke ranks and stampeded in the direction from which they'd come.

Braddock heard the shooting and knew what it meant. Calmly, like a true professional, he halted the main body to straighten the ranks and give final instructions. Then, with George Washington at his side, he rode toward the battle.

The column had gone only a quarter mile when remnants of the advance guard appeared ahead. They were running and so frightened that they ignored even the general's command to halt. All they knew was that death was behind them and that their comrades' ranks offered a hiding place. Without pausing, they pushed into the carefully aligned ranks, shattering their order and spreading confusion. Just then, Sir Peter Halket arrived with the second division and the supply train. Instead of halting when he saw the confusion ahead, he ordered it forward at top speed. Soon the advance guard, main force, artillery, ammunition wagons, and packhorses were bunched together on the narrow trail.

Dumas's men blazed away from the front and sides of the milling mass. Hundreds of Indians fired from *above,* from a hilltop overlooking the trail. The redcoats were twenty deep in places, an impossible target to miss. Individual bullets often passed through the heads of two men before lodging in that of a third. Soldiers pitched forward, adding their blood to the rivulets flowing along the ground. Bodies piled up in heaps.

The redcoats were no longer soldiers but an armed mob, more dangerous to themselves than to the enemy. With so much happening at once, it became difficult for one to focus, to regain self-control. Riderless horses, their mouths foaming and eyes filled with terror, reared and plunged through the mob. The screams of the wounded mingled with the crash of musketry and Indian war whoops. It felt as if the world had suddenly gone insane.

Death was everywhere, yet the senders of death remained under cover and never showed themselves; few survivors remembered seeing an enemy during that whole day. All that the redcoats could see were orange flashes through the gray fog of battle. Clouds of gunsmoke hung close to the ground, making them sneeze and bringing tears to their eyes. Redcoats mechanically loaded their muskets and fired without aiming. Many guns went off while pointed skyward; others mowed down other redcoats at the front of the mass.

Braddock's one hope lay in dispersing his troops behind trees and rocks. It would have been worth the gamble, for they were goners in the open; besides, they still outnumbered the enemy, who were in no position to trade them shot for shot. The Indians, who never stood up to a determined foe, would probably have faded into the woods, leaving the French to retreat on their own or die at their posts.

Braddock, unfortunately, couldn't imagine that way of fighting. He'd learned his trade on the battlefields of Europe, and he'd learned it well—*too well*. Honorable men weren't savages. They had always fought in the open, in close order. When Washington begged Braddock to allow his men to fight Indian-style, he refused.

The Virginians began to take matters into their own hands. Several groups took cover, only to be cut down when regulars mistook them for Indians. An entire unit was wiped out this way, every man shot in the back.

Redcoats who took cover were roughly handled. "Where the hell are you going?" the general shouted. "Get back there!

Get back in these ranks and fight like men, not animals. Form lines, captains!" Braddock and his officers rode in among them and beat them with the flats of their swords. The men returned to the ranks, where they continued to fall in heaps.

Braddock's courage never failed. With bullets snapping around his ears, he galloped his horse into the thick of the fight. Four horses were shot from under him, but he always managed to find another mount.

George Washington was every bit as courageous as his general. He rode all over, exposing himself to danger at every turn. His horse fell dead, hurling him over the saddle, but he sprang to his feet and leaped into the saddle of another as it ran past. This mount also caught a bullet, and he found yet another. He'd just ridden off when he felt a tugging at his back; four bullets ripped through his coat but left him unscratched.

By now, nothing could change the outcome of the battle. After three hours of fighting, sixty-three out of eighty-six officers lay dead or wounded. William Shirley, son of the Massachusetts governor, fell with a bullet in the brain. Another bullet tore into the breast of Sir Peter Halket. His son, a lieutenant, rushed to his side. As he lifted his father's head, a bullet carried away the back of his skull. Father and son lay still, embracing each other in death.

At last Braddock realized that he had been defeated. He stood in the stirrups and cupped his hands to his mouth. "Retreat! Retreat!" he cried. "Back to the river and cross it. Retreat!" It was the most painful order he'd ever given. And it would be his last.

Braddock was turning in the saddle when he felt a sting in his right arm. The sting was followed by the searing pain of a bullet cutting through his lungs. Frothy blood poured from his mouth as he toppled to the ground. Some passing soldiers tossed their dying general into a cart and rejoined the stampede back across the Monongahela. Daniel Boone and other wagon drivers

*General Braddock, fatally wounded, was tossed into a wagon by his
retreating troops. When he died four days later, George Washington had his
body buried in the middle of the road; the army then marched over the
grave to conceal it from the scalp-hunting Indians.*

had already cut their horses' traces and ridden out of the path of
the mob.

The Battle of the Wilderness, or Braddock's Defeat, surprised everyone. For the English, it was a disaster pure and
simple. Of the fourteen hundred who had marched with Braddock's division, fewer than five hundred escaped unharmed. All
the others were either dead, prisoners, or wounded. For the

French, it was a victory beyond their wildest dreams. At a cost of thirty dead and as many wounded, they had crushed a major enemy offensive. Nothing like it had ever happened in Europe.

The fight meant glory and treasure for the Indians. The battlefield was littered with loot: guns, bayonets, canteens, helmets, and the thousand other things a defeated army leaves behind. There were also scalps. Many scalps.

Braves moved among the corpses, lifting scalps and whooping as they held up the bloody trophies. The shrieks of the wounded were horrible, as tomahawks or war clubs smashed their skulls. They were lucky, for they died quickly. Captives were stripped naked, their hands tied, and their faces and chests smudged with charcoal. The Canadians knew this as the *cut-ta-ho-tha*—the mark of the condemned. That night they were slowly roasted on the bank of the Allegheny opposite Fort Duquesne. It wasn't till sunup that their screams stopped and the chirping of birds could be heard.

Braddock's dead were never buried. Bears ate their remains and, it was said, lost their fear of humans. The skeletons eventually disintegrated and vanished into the earth.

The remnants of Braddock's army stumbled along the trail to join the second division under Colonel Thomas Dunbar. The general lingered through four days of pain and shame. "Who would have thought it?" he moaned. Washington, he admitted, had been right to want to fight Indian-style. "We shall better know how to deal with them next time."

But there would be no "next time" for Edward Braddock. He died near Fort Necessity, and Washington had him buried in the middle of the trail. Troops, horses, and wagons then passed over the grave, erasing all sign of it to prevent the Indians from finding and mutilating his body.

Colonel Dunbar wrote the final page in Braddock's Defeat. As the highest-ranking officer still fit for duty, he ordered most of the wagons and supplies burned. Cannon, hauled over the mountains with such effort, were spiked. Gunpowder barrels were broken open and their contents scattered to the winds. When he'd finished the destruction, Dunbar marched for Fort Cumberland and then to Philadelphia. It was midsummer, but he announced that the army was going into winter quarters.

B R A D D O C K ' S   D E F E A T cost Great Britain more than lives and land. It cost her the colonists' respect. Americans, already outraged over the return of Louisbourg, began to have doubts about the regulars. Words like "cowardice" and "stupidity" were often heard in the months after July 1755. George Washington wrote in a private letter: "Our Virginians behaved like men and died like soldiers," mostly at the hands of their allies. As for the redcoats, "those cowardly dogs of soldiers," they deserved the contempt of decent people.

Washington was the only officer who gained from the disaster. His courage and good sense made him a celebrity in the colonies. Suddenly his name became a household word. A minister spoke for many when he noted that God had saved "that heroic youth," because one day he would do "some important service [for] his country."

The colonists also paid a high price for the defeat. Colonel Dunbar's decision to go into winter quarters early left the western borders unprotected. The colonial governors knew what that meant and protested. But nothing they said could change Dunbar's mind. He was sorry, he said, but the frontier people would have to fend for themselves.

Captain Dumas, who had replaced Contrecoeur as commander of Fort Duquesne, saw the colonists' weaknesses and decided to act. He called the chiefs to a council and, as they drank brandy, passed around the red hatchet. They took it, not only out of greed for loot and scalps, but because they wanted to keep the land-hungry English out of the Ohio country.

"Go out," Dumas told them. "Spread yourselves through the whole country as far as you can go. Take scalps. Kill the English, all of them. Kill them in any way you like—with club or gun, knife or tomahawk. Torture them with fire and coals. Burn their houses, destroy their livestock, destroy all they own. Drive them back to the sea-cities, and there our armies will come and finish the destruction. Kill them!"

And they did.

French and Indian war parties freely crossed the Alleghenies for the next two years. Filtering through the forests on the eastern slopes, they struck without warning or pity. The raiders left a belt of death and destruction forty miles wide in places along the western borders of Pennsylvania, Maryland, and Virginia. "They kill all they meet," wrote a French priest who'd seen them in action.

In the language of the frontier, there was scarcely "a dry settlement" along the border, seldom a night without "blood on the moon." Settlements became wastelands, abandoned to the forest and the wolves. By the fall of 1755, war parties had penetrated to within fifty miles of Philadelphia. Conditions became so bad that some settlers brought wagonloads of their murdered kinsmen to town and left them on the steps of the Pennsylvania Assembly building.

The colonies tried to defend themselves without the British army. It wasn't easy. George Washington, who had been given command of the Virginia frontier, found his task an ordeal from start to finish. There were never enough supplies or men to use them. Militiamen, concerned about their own farms and families, constantly deserted; some units always had at least one-third of their manpower "over the hill." Washington promised a thousand lashes to first-time deserters and built a gallows forty feet

This old print shows the horrors of a typical Indian raid on the Pennsylvania frontier of the 1750s.

high to hang repeated offenders. Both punishments were used, but desertions continued.

Washington nearly lost faith in himself during those awful years of frontier duty. The sights he saw, the cries he heard, were heartbreaking and he felt so helpless. "But what can I do?" he wrote Governor Dinwiddie. "The . . . tears of the women and . . . petitions of the men melt me in such deadly sorrow that I solemnly declare (that) I could offer myself a willing sacrifice to the butchering enemy provided that would contribute to the people's ease. . . . I would be a willing offering to savage fury, and die by inches to save the people."

Gradually, Washington and other colonial leaders organized a defense system. Not all of these leaders, however, had military training. Benjamin Franklin was more comfortable in a library than in an armed camp. Yet he had a gift that any professional soldier could admire: He knew how to inspire others with his enthusiasm. Franklin recruited a regiment of volunteers on his own. He was so popular with them that they saluted him with volleys of musketry in front of his house. So many shots were fired that the vibrations shattered some of the glassware used in his electrical experiments.

Each colony built a chain of forts every twenty or thirty miles along the eastern slopes of the Alleghenies. These forts guarded key points such as passes and were manned by paid troops. It is no accident that so many American cities have "fort" in their name. Forts were havens for the people in dangerous times. After the danger passed, the forts remained to become centers of settlement and trade.

"Fort" became a basic word in the frontiersman's vocabulary. Government forts were backed up by "private forts," hundreds of log cabins, mills, and churches turned into strongpoints. Any building could be "forted" by shuttering the windows, drilling loopholes at different levels, and lining the inner walls with sandbags to make them bulletproof. A deep cellar sheltered families and served as a fireproof storeroom.

Settlers learned always to be on guard, always ready for trouble. Relatives and neighbors went to the fields together. While some worked, others watched from behind trees or scouted the woods. A worker always kept his musket close at hand.

The alarm could sound at any time. A scout might gallop by on horseback to alert isolated settlements that Indians had been sighted. Smoke signals by day, or huge bonfires to light up the night sky, carried the alert over a wide area quickly.

When a settler and his family "forted," rushed to the nearest stronghold, everyone knew what to do when they arrived. Men and teenaged boys stood by loopholes with muskets. Women and older girls sat on the floor behind their menfolk. Their job was to reload guns and to make bullets by melting lead bars and pouring the metal into bullet molds. Smaller children stood near the water barrels, ready to douse any fire arrows that might come through the windows. The smallest children stayed out of the way in the cellar. Axes, knives, and clubs lay nearby in case of hand-to-hand fighting. Settlers were determined to sell their lives dearly. They might die, but they would die fighting. Most times, Indians would sooner knock down hornets' nests than go after stubbornly defended strongholds.

Colonial governments also formed special units known as "ranging companies." Rangers, as their members were called, were usually expert hunters who made a career of Indian fighting. Like today's Green Berets and commandos, they specialized in long-distance patrols and raids in enemy territory. The purpose of their raids was to keep the enemy off balance so that he wouldn't be able to attack the frontier settlements.

To fight Indians, rangers had to become like Indians. This meant traveling light, moving swiftly, and keeping out of sight. Rangers wore moccasins, walked "Indian file," and wore camouflaged clothing: buckskin breeches and jackets that blended with the forest and made them invisible. Rangers carried light packs, for they knew how to live off the land. Their weapons were ideal for forest fighting. They carried short muskets with blackened barrels to prevent glints in the sun. Tomahawks and scalping knives were thrust into their belts. To avoid ambush, they never traveled the same trail returning. If attacked, they had none of the regulars' prejudice against taking cover. The commander cried, "Tree all!" and everyone dove for cover.

Rangers turned the tables on the enemy, changing him from

the hunter into the hunted. When patrolling, rangers followed Benjamin Franklin's advice about using packs of fierce dogs to flush out Indians. He suggested that they keep their dogs on slip-strings to prevent them from tiring themselves out unnecessarily. When they came to a suspicious area, two or three of the best trackers should be released. If they found anyone hiding, the whole pack was turned loose. Enemies who weren't torn to bits were shot; few ever escaped with their lives.

Rangers were merciless to Indians. The horrors of frontier warfare had hardened them, made them bloodthirsty. Many said, "The only good Indian is a dead Indian." And they acted on their belief. If they found an Indian encampment, they'd attack when everyone slept; Indian camps were easy to surprise, for they seldom put out guards at night, particularly in winter. The rangers struck, killed, and vanished into the wilderness. Left behind were bodies and scalps tacked to trees.

By 1757, the combination of forts and rangers had checked Dumas's raiders. And by then it was difficult to find a frontiersman with a good word to say about the British regulars.

AMONG THE LOOT from Braddock's Defeat was a cart with the general's personal possessions, including a small camp desk. The redcoats had fled in such disorder that nobody had remembered to burn the desk's contents. That was a mistake, for in one of the drawers the French found a complete set of British campaign plans.

Marquis Pierre de Vaudreuil, Duquesne's replacement as governor, smiled as he leafed through the documents. Here was a priceless treasure! Like his father, who had ruled Canada during Queen Anne's War, he believed in seizing every opportunity to harm an enemy. Although British forces were larger, knowing their plans loaded the odds in favor of the French.

Vaudreuil began by rushing reinforcements to Fort Niagara. He needn't have bothered, since the English proved to be their own worst enemy. Governor Shirley delayed his advance so long, and his men became so discouraged at the news of Braddock's Defeat, that the expedition never got under way.

Shirley did better against the Acadians. After Acadia became British in 1713, it was renamed Nova Scotia—New Scotland—and the port of Halifax built as a forward base against Louisbourg. The people, who still called themselves Acadians, were simple farmers and fishermen. Few conquered peoples have ever been treated so generously. In order to win their loyalty, the British government gave them privileges unknown in any European country or colony. They paid no taxes and were excused from militia service; their Protestant rulers even allowed them to practice their Catholic faith in peace.

Although the Acadians had lived under the British flag for forty years, their hearts were still French. Again and again they refused to take an oath of loyalty to Great Britain. They prayed instead that a French army would return one day to drive out the British.

Now, in 1755, with full-scale warfare about to begin, the Acadians were seen as traitors. The English feared that an assault from Louisbourg would be supported by an Acadian rebellion, forcing them to fight on two fronts at once. To prevent this, the Acadians had to be driven from their land.

During the summer, Shirley sent thirty-six ships and two thousand militiamen to Nova Scotia. It was a nasty assignment, but a necessary one, the troops believed. Patrols hustled the people into their stone churches to hear officers read the expulsion order. People wept and spoke bitterly about injustice. It was no use; the time for talking had passed.

Troops scoured the countryside to destroy the people's means of earning a living. Homes and barns went up in flames; crops were burned in the fields and cattle seized. Six thousand

Acadian men, women, and children were driven aboard the ships at gunpoint for a journey—where?

To send them to Canada or France would have strengthened the enemy. To send them to Great Britain would have burdened the British taxpayer with their support. The only thing to do was to scatter them among the thirteen colonies.

Few welcomed them, but neither were they harmed. In some places, colonists fed them and helped them start new lives. Eventually most Acadians adopted English ways, just as captured English people became Indians or Canadians. Several hundred reached Louisiana, where their descendants, the "Cajuns," live today.

BRADDOCK'S PAPERS revealed that he meant to capture Crown Point, or Scalp Point, as the Indians called it. Crown Point commanded the best inland waterway from New York City to Canada; the Hudson River–Lake Champlain route.

One could sail up the Hudson to a place only fifteen miles from Lake George. Here was "the Great Carrying Place," a portage trail through the hills to the lakeside. From there, a short boat ride brought you across the lake to another portage trail around rapids that flowed into Lake Champlain. Once you left the Champlain shore, it was smooth sailing up the lake to the Richelieu River and then into the St. Lawrence to within forty miles of Montreal.

A British officer reads the decree expelling the Acadians. After living many years under British rule, these farmers in Nova Scotia were driven from their homes because they refused to swear an oath of loyalty to Great Britain. The poet Henry Wadsworth Longfellow later wrote of their sufferings in Evangeline.

The Hudson-Champlain route was a dagger with Crown Point as its handle. French control of it menaced the New York colony and western New England. English control made it easy to stab into the Canadian heartland. It was the French, however, who first saw Crown Point's importance. In 1731, they built Fort St. Frèdèric at Crown Point on the heights above the western shore of Lake Champlain. Nobody could pass beneath the fort's guns without permission from the king of France.

Braddock chose William Johnson to lead the expedition against Crown Point. Johnson was one of the most important men in the colonies. As a young immigrant from Ireland, he had settled in the Mohawk Valley, where he began to trade with the Five Nations. Tall and red-faced, with sparkling eyes and a broad smile, he earned the Indians' respect. Johnson never broke a promise, never cheated or traded shoddy goods. He learned the Indians' language, laughed at their jokes, and danced their dances dressed in moccasins and breechcloth. They were always welcome at Johnson Hall, his sprawling mansion on the banks of the Mohawk. Hundreds of tribesmen could be seen at any time camped in the gardens or asleep in their blankets in the hallways.

Indian women adored him. Frontier legend said that Johnson had fathered over a hundred half-breed children. Perhaps. We do know that the mother of eight of his children was the sister of a Mohawk sachem. Known as "the brown Lady Johnson," she was his wife in all but name. Her Mohawk kinsmen made him a war chief and called him Warraghiyagey—"He Who Does Much Business."

Johnson used his business skills to raise an army of three thousand New Yorkers and New Englanders, plus about five hundred Mohawks, for the drive on Crown Point. Except for a few officers who had been at Louisbourg ten years earlier, his troops were farmers, shopkeepers, and craftsmen who had never been in combat. Captain William Eyre was his artillery commander and the only redcoat to serve with the expedition. Eyre was

Sir William Johnson was one of the few Englishmen trusted by the Indians, especially the tribes of the Five Nations.

in charge of eleven cannon, among them two thirty-two-pounders that fired iron balls six inches in diameter.

Meantime, a powerful French force was gliding over Lake Champlain toward Crown Point. Its commander was Baron Ludwig August Dieskau, a German who had served the French for many years. Dieskau's thirty-two-hundred-man army consisted of regulars, Caughnawaga and Abnaki. Although outnumbered and without artillery, Dieskau felt confident, for one French regular, he believed, was worth three of Johnson's colonials.

Johnson's army gathered at Albany and moved up the Hudson River in boats and along the shore until it came to where the river turned sharply west. Here, at the entry to the Great Carrying Place, he began Fort Edward, named for a grandson of King George II. After leaving five hundred men to guard the fort, he moved the army to a campsite near the southern shore of Lake George, which he named in the king's honor. His plan was to advance northward in stages, guarding his supply line and line of retreat every step of the way. He had no idea that the enemy knew his plans and that Dieskau's army was nearby.

Dieskau had been watching his movements through the eyes of his scouts. His plan was both simple and deadly: He meant to launch a surprise attack in overwhelming strength against Fort Edward. Once the fort fell, Johnson's lifeline would be cut, forcing him to surrender or starve in the wilderness.

Scouts from both sides soon changed their generals' plans. Johnson's Mohawks found enemy tracks in the woods around Fort Edward. That news must have come as a shock to him, for he now broke one of the basic rules of warfare: never split your army without knowing the enemy's exact position. Colonel Ephriam Williams was ordered to take a thousand men to find the French camp and destroy it.

Old Hendrick, a Mohawk chief and friend of Johnson's, wasn't happy. "If those thousand are to be killed, they are too

Old Hendrick, a famous Mohawk sachem loyal to the English, was killed in an ambush near Fort Edward. There are thirty-nine crosses carved on the tree behind him, each standing for an enemy killed, scalped, or captured.

many," he said, "and if they are to fight, they are too few. My warriors who saw the trail they left say there are many more in the war party than you will send against them." But when Johnson insisted upon going ahead with the plan, Old Hendrick gave in, although he feared the worst.

The detachment left camp at dawn, September 8, 1755. An hour later, a breathless scout reported its departure to Dieskau. The baron knew what had to be done. Swiftly, silently, he positioned his army along both sides of the portage road north of Fort Edward. This done, he waited for the English to walk into the trap.

It was midmorning when the column, Colonel Williams and Old Hendrick leading on horseback, rounded a bend in the road. All was still, except for the snapping of twigs. Suddenly a doe and two fawns bolted out of the woods, stood in the road for a moment, and then disappeared into the woods on the other side. Hunters among the English were wondering what, or *who*, had frightened them . . . when it happened.

The woods exploded.

A storm of bullets tore through the column from either side of the road. Scores of men dropped without knowing what hit them, including Colonel Williams. Old Hendrick crawled under a tree with a big hole in his chest. The last thing he saw were braves coming toward him with scalping knives.

Back at camp, Johnson heard shots and ordered drummers to sound the alert. Men ran for their weapons. Wagons were hastily overturned and logs rolled into place to form a low barricade. Captain Eyre trained his cannon on the road.

Within a half hour, the first of hundreds of fugitives came running down the road, many bleeding and hysterical. Johnson's men caught their comrades' hysteria and began to leave their posts. Had the enemy arrived then, nothing could have stopped them. It would have been another Braddock's Defeat, only worse, because more men were involved. But Dieskau's men were no-where to be seen.

The baron was having his own troubles. No sooner had he destroyed Williams's detachment when his Indians began argu-ing and pointing muskets at one another. Some Abnaki had cap-tured three Mohawks and were preparing to burn them when the Caughnawaga insisted that their cousins be spared. Dieskau ar-rived in the nick of time to prevent a fight. It took lots of persuad-ing, but he finally convinced them to deal with the prisoners after the battle. Still, an hour had been lost, time Johnson's officers used to calm their men and to improve their defenses.

The Canadians and Indians burst from the woods on either side of the waiting English camp. In front, facing the barricade, were the French regulars. They stood in three long lines, one behind the other, bayonets glinting in the sun.

At Dieskau's signal, the first rank fired. The volley sounded like the crack of doom, but it was only the beginning. As the front rank knelt to reload, the other two ranks stepped forward. The second rank, now the first, fired, then it, too, knelt to give the third rank a chance. In this way, the regulars kept up a continuous fire.

Captain Eyre's cannon thundered in reply. His guns were loaded not with solid shot, but "canister," canvas bags filled with musket balls. They had become giant shotguns.

A hailstorm of lead burst upon the tightly packed ranks. Each time the guns fired, more white coats became streaked with red. Gradually, the huddled colonials peered over their barricade and, seeing Frenchmen fall, began to fire their rifles.

This wasn't what the Caughnawaga and Abnaki had ex-pected. Suddenly they ran to the edge of the forest, out of gun-shot range, and squatted on their haunches. They had had enough fighting for today. Now they would watch the whites maul each other.

Dieskau was running toward the Indians to rally them, when

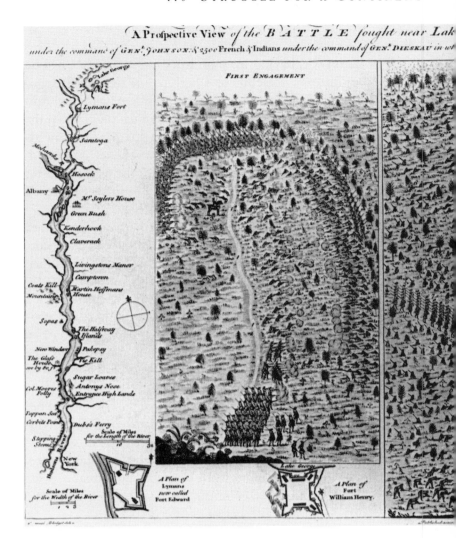

Samuel Blodgett's "Perspective Plan of the Battle Near Lake George, 1755," was drawn by an eyewitness to William Johnson's defeat of the army of Baron Dieskau.

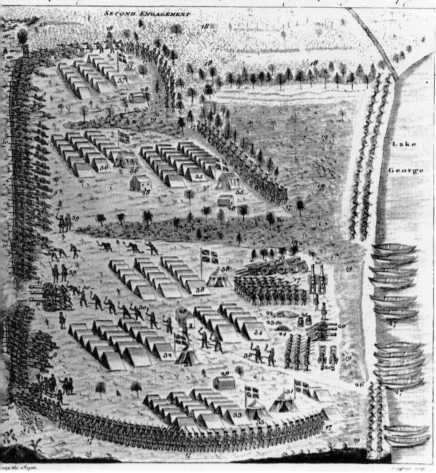

the 8th of Sep. 1755. between 2000 English with 250 Mohawks,
victorious captivating the French Gen. with a Number of his Men killing 700 & putting the rest to flight

SECOND ENGAGEMENT

Lake

George

a bullet shattered his knee and he fell on his face. He was rising on his elbows when two more slugs found him, one burying itself in his backside.

"Take command!" he shouted to Captain Montreuil, his

second-in-command. "Take command! I'll be all right!" But it was already too late. With Dieskau down and the Indians out of the fight, the regulars began to falter.

This was just what Johnson's officers wanted to see. "At them! Up and at them!" they shouted, waving their swords and pointing toward the regulars.

First in small groups, then as a human wave, the colonials leaped the barricade and charged. In the hand-to-hand fighting that followed, men went at each other with gun butts and hatchets, bayonets and bare hands. At last the French regulars broke and ran.

A squad of New Englanders found Dieskau under a tree and, not knowing if he was armed, shot him again. The baron didn't know how long he'd been unconscious when he awoke in a tent. Men were arguing near his cot in Iroquoian and, yes, English with an Irish brogue.

"What do they want?" he asked after the Indians stormed out of the tent.

"To burn you, by God, eat you, and smoke you in their pipes, in revenge for three or four of their chiefs that were killed," replied William Johnson. "But never fear; you shall be safe with me, or else they shall kill us both." With that, Dieskau lay back on his cot, glad to be alive and the prisoner of such a man.

Johnson, too, was pleased with himself. He had recovered on the shore of Lake George some of the British honor lost near the Monongahela. He had also made history. For the first time, American amateurs—amateur officers, amateur soldiers—had whipped European professionals on a battlefield. It would not be the last time.

Both armies had had enough fighting for one season. Johnson, seeing that he couldn't advance farther, began building a fort alongside the portage road at the southern end of Lake George. He named it Fort William Henry in honor of King George's second grandson.

The French also dug in. Dieskau's army retreated to Crown Point and began work on another fort ten miles to the south, where Lake George joins Lake Champlain. They called it Fort Carillon—"the Place of the Chorus of Bells"—because the lapping of water against the shore mingling with the wind in the trees reminded them of distant chimes. That fort would become famous in our history under its Indian name: Ticonderoga.

Carpenters were still working on their forts when news came next summer that England and France had declared war on May 18, 1756. At last it was official. The war that George Washington had begun now became worldwide. Englishmen knew it as the Great War for the Empire, Europeans as the Seven Years' War. Americans called it the French and Indian War.

⇶ IV ⇷

Montcalm

O N M A Y 11, 1756, a squadron of French warships had nosed into the Gulf of St. Lawrence. It had been a rough voyage, complete with icebergs, storms, and a narrow escape from a superior British fleet. But they had come through all right, and now the twelve hundred regulars, ashen faced from seasickness, crowded the rails for their first glimpse of the New World. The declaration of war, they knew, was coming, and they were curious about the land in which so many of them would leave their bones.

Aboard the flagship *Licorne,* a man in a white uniform trimmed with gold paced the quarterdeck alone. He hardly noticed the forests slipping by on either side, for his thoughts were far away. It was springtime at home, too, and he missed his wife and children. God, he wished he could be with them at Candiac, the family estate, with its rolling fields and neat orchards. But when duty called, he, Louis Joseph, marquis de Montcalm, had always answered. And now it called him to lead the forces of His Majesty, King Louis XV, in the American wilderness.

Montcalm at forty-four was a small, lean, restless man with

is Joseph M.is de MONTCALM GOZON ,
9 fevrier 1712 + 14 Septembre 1759 .

The Marquis de Montcalm, one of France's outstanding generals of the
eighteenth century, defeated the British in several important engagements
in North America.

a long nose and large black eyes. "Lively as a squirrel," friends called him, because he seemed unable to sit still for more than a few minutes at a time. He spoke rapidly, as if his tongue must race double-time to keep up with his thoughts.

"War is the grave of the Montcalms" was an ancient family saying, possibly as old as France itself. The men of his family had been fighting their country's battles since the Middle Ages, and some had paid the supreme price in every generation. Louis Joseph, a soldier since age fourteen, was a veteran of countless battles and skirmishes, having served through some of the hardest fighting of the War of the Austrian Succession. His body bore the marks of his courage and good luck. A round scar left by a musket ball was visible on his forehead. Saber slashes had left four long scars on his chest and back; they ached when the weather turned cold and damp. He always remembered to thank God for the near misses, just as he always remembered the family saying.

Montcalm had come to Canada with a three-part mission. He was, first, to reinforce the water routes linking Canada to the West. Second, any British forces that threatened these routes were to be destroyed. Finally, he must repel attacks on Canada from whatever direction they came. In all this, it was most important to remain friendly with the Indians.

Montcalm's chief officers were as fine as could be found in any army. They were a joy to work with—loyal, dependable, fearless. Brigadier General Gaston de Lévis, his second-in-command, was a brilliant soldier who could be counted upon to do anything humanly possible. Captain Louis Antoine de Bougainville, Montcalm's personal aide, later became one of France's greatest seamen. He commanded the first French expedition around the world, discovered Bougainville Island in the South Pacific, and fought alongside the patriots during the American Revolution. His diary is the best eyewitness account we have of Montcalm's campaigns.

Montcalm's first objective was Oswego, an English outpost on Lake Ontario. The Oswego River flows north into the lake here. On the river's eastern bank, the English had built Fort Ontario, a star-shaped structure of wood and earth; two smaller forts, Oswego and George, lay across the river.

Oswego had been a problem for thirty years. In peacetime, it acted as a magnet to draw the fur trade of the western Great Lakes away from Montreal. Now that France and England were at war, it endangered France's position in the Ohio country. Ships built on the lakeside and based at Oswego could cut communications between the St. Lawrence, Lake Erie, and the chain of posts between Fort Niagara and New Orleans.

Raiding parties constantly prowled the woods around Oswego in search of English victims. Woodcutting parties from the forts often failed to return. Boatmen on the Oswego River became used to seeing heads impaled on stakes planted along the banks. Sentries were scalped. One soldier got drunk and wandered into the woods, where he fell asleep under a tree. He returned next morning, sober and wide awake, but without his scalp. He couldn't say when or how he'd lost it, but otherwise he was healthy.

Montcalm, however, meant to do more than scalp drunkards. He left Montreal late in July 1756 with 3,000 men, mostly regulars, and 250 Indians in a fleet of bateaux, large flat-bottomed rowboats. He brought along a train of powerful artillery, some of which had belonged to Braddock's army. Barring accidents, he expected to win without much of a fight.

Montcalm's oarsmen paddled day and night for two weeks; the troops got used to aching legs and to sleeping in canoes. On August 13, the army landed a few miles east of Fort Ontario and began carving a trail through the woods. When Colonel Mercer, the English commander, learned that the invaders had heavy cannons, he decided to abandon the fort: Its wooden walls could never withstand a siege, and there was no point in losing lives needlessly. That night, he had the fort's few small guns spiked and ferried the garrison across the river to Fort Oswego. Even so, he knew that the English position was hopeless. If help didn't arrive in a day or two, he would have to surrender or face a general massacre.

Next morning, the French opened fire with every gun from across the river. The walls of Fort Oswego began to splinter and fly apart as the iron balls slammed home. Colonel Mercer was directing the defense from the top of a wall when a ball hit him in the stomach and cut him in half. At the sight of his mangled remains, the garrison's courage vanished. Moments later, a white sheet was run up the flagpole. Forts Oswego and George surrendered on Montcalm's promise of kind treatment.

The general had given *his* word, but that didn't bind the Indians. No sooner were the gates opened than braves burst into the forts and began tomahawking the English wounded. A hundred died, twice those killed in the bombardment. It took every ounce of Montcalm's energy to calm his allies; only promises of gifts made them release others marked for death.

Oswego taught Montcalm a lesson. He learned that the Indians, though invaluable as allies, didn't obey orders like European regulars. And that knowledge made him worry as much about his friends as his enemies.

Oswego was systematically looted. Everything of value— food, tools, clothes, even fishnets—was loaded onto bateaux and sent to Montreal with the prisoners. When the forts and storehouses were empty, they were burned. A few days later, English scouts found the site covered with ashes, rubble, and rotting corpses.

News of Montcalm's victory spread like wildfire among the tribes; they heard of him even in the land of the redwoods on the shore of the western ocean. Painted warriors gathered around campfires to tell of the *Onontio*, the mighty war chief who had arisen among the French. Fearless and wise, he could see into all things, even into the future. He was so tall, they whispered, that he walked with his head lost in the clouds; when he stamped his foot, the earth trembled and forts crumbled to dust. The next time he called, the tribes would rush to fight under his banner.

HAVING REMOVED the threat from Oswego, Montcalm took his regiments to Lake Champlain. Much work still remained to be done there before he could carry the war down the Hudson Valley to New York City. Fort St. Frédéric had to be strengthened and Fort Carillon completed. During the rest of 1756 and into the spring of 1757, his whitecoats put aside their muskets for picks and shovels, hammers and saws.

As the work neared completion, messengers were sent to invite the tribes to a war council at Ticonderoga. Montcalm already had eight thousand French troops, regulars, and Canadians, but they weren't enough for what he had in mind.

Montcalm's fame drew Indians to him. At least two thousand braves from forty-one tribes took up the red hatchet at his request. Some came from so far away that no other Indians, let alone Frenchmen, understood their languages. There were Winnebago from Wisconsin and Iowa from west of the Mississippi. Shawnee and Delaware, Miami and Peoria poured in from the Ohio country and beyond. Ottawa, Chippewa, Huron, Nipissing, and Menominee were there. The longhouses of the Five Nations sent small bands of Cayuga and Oneida, Onandega and Seneca; they had lost confidence in the English and many of their young men wanted to join a winner. Only William Johnson's Mohawk stood by the English to a man.

Captain Bougainville was shocked when he visited the campsites around Ticonderoga. He had seen Indians before, but never such strange people as those from the Far West. "They go naked, excepting a strip of cloth passed through a belt, and paint themselves black, red, blue, and other colors," he wrote in his diary. "Their heads are shaved and adorned with bunches of feathers and they wear rings of brass wire in their ears. They wear beaver-skin blankets and carry lances, bows and arrows and quivers made from the skins of beasts. For the rest, they are straight, well made, and generally very tall. Their religion is brute paganism."

A council was held at night around a roaring bonfire. War chiefs, scores of them, sat cross-legged on the ground, their eyes fixed on the small figure in white and gold. Their speaker, Pennahouel, an Ottawa with skin like wrinkled leather, welcomed the famous *Onontio*. His people had heard wondrous tales of Montcalm's size and power. "But you are a little man, my father. It is when we look into your eyes that we can see the strength and greatness of the pine tree and the spirit and courage of the eagle."

"*Ho! Ho! Ho! Ho!*" Pennahouel's fellow chiefs muttered in agreement.

Montcalm rose and began to speak slowly so that his Canadian interpreter could translate every word. He explained that his father, King Louis XV, had sent him to save his red children from English greed. To do this, Fort William Henry had to be destroyed along with everyone in it who dared to resist.

Montcalm was describing his plans when suddenly a giant tree groaned, shook, and fell with a crash that echoed through the forest. The noise excited the Indians, who believed it was a sign from the spirits foretelling the future. But what did the future hold? What would fall, the English fort or the French cause? Montcalm's plan hung by a thread. Let the Indians once get the idea that the fallen tree was a spirit-warning, and they'd leave him flat. The quick-thinking general smiled, raised his hands to heaven, and spoke.

"My children! See! As the tree has fallen, so, too, will the English fall before us!"

As the Indians shouted and whooped their approval, an aide brought Montcalm a package. Slowly, deliberately, he began to draw out its contents. The Indians fell silent, holding their breath at the sight.

Montcalm held a huge belt of wampum made of six thousand beads. No brave had ever seen anything so beautiful or so precious.

Everyone knew the meaning of its design. It pledged peace and unity among the tribes and their French brothers—and death to their English foes. Montcalm held the belt toward Pennahouel, who accepted it in the name of his fellow chiefs.

The logs of the bonfire snapped, crackled, and hissed. Sparks shot into the velvety blackness of the sky.

Drums began to throb and a thousand warriors rose. Slowly, then faster and faster until their heads reeled, they lost themselves in the war dance. Tomahawks flashed in the firelight. Muskets cracked. Braves danced and sang and whooped until the morning star appeared in the east. And then they took to the warpath.

The English knew that trouble was brewing, but they had no way of learning Montcalm's strength or intentions. French and Indian patrols had turned the woods south of Fort Carillon into a killing ground. English scouting parties were tracked, trapped, and wiped out to the last man.

Lieutenant Marin ambushed a 32-man party within sight of Fort Edward; although they surrendered, it never entered Marin's mind to take prisoners, who might slow his movements. Another party, 350 men in canoes, fell victim to a water ambush on Lake George. They had rounded a point of land when hundreds of hidden canoes darted out from the shore. They never had a chance. Desperate men dove overboard in an effort to swim to safety. It was hopeless, for the Indians in their canoes speared them like fish. Fewer than a hundred escaped; all the others were killed outright or roasted alive at Ticonderoga. In effect, Montcalm's patrols had blinded the enemy.

Major General Daniel Webb, Johnson's successor on the upper Hudson, ignored these warnings. The redcoat officer felt sure that he could handle anything. Manpower certainly wasn't a problem, he believed. In addition to thirty-two hundred regulars and militia with him at Fort Edward, Colonel George Monro had another twenty-two hundred at Fort William Henry. That fort could take care of itself. Its guns—large and small cannons, swivels, mortars—could stand up to anything but the heaviest artillery. The place was so crowded that eighteen hundred men had to be stationed in an entrenched camp nearby. Reinforcements would have been more of a problem than a help in these circumstances.

The French left Ticonderoga in three divisions on July 30, 1757. Since there weren't enough boats for the whole army, Lévis, still second-in-command, marched with three thousand men along the western shore of Lake George; the Indians moved through the woods on their own secret trails. Montcalm sailed with the regulars and the supplies. The artillery rafts rode low in the water, for they carried some of the heaviest cannon in North America.

Bougainville wasn't happy. It wasn't that he didn't expect victory; that was guaranteed by the cannon. But, a few days earlier, several chiefs had come to Montcalm's tent. "Father," said one, "do not expect that we can easily give quarter to the English. We have young men who have never yet drunk of this broth [blood]. Fresh meat has brought them here from the ends of the earth. It is most necessary that they learn to wield the knife and plunge it into the English heart."

Bougainville, an honorable man and a good soldier, had learned warfare in Europe. The men he'd served with never killed prisoners, much less ate them and drank their blood. The Indians' words sent a chill up his spine. He was afraid for the English and, even more, for French honor.

Montcalm easily surrounded Fort William Henry and isolated the entrenched camp. For nearly a week, his big guns pounded the walls, knocking holes in them in many places. The fort's defenders, many of whom were weak and recovering from smallpox, worked frantically to close the breaches. At night, when the French guns fell silent, they repaired the damage with timbers and sandbags, only to see their hard work blown away in the morning. It was a losing fight.

One day, an Indian brought Montcalm a letter found on the body of an Englishman ambushed in the woods. It was General Webb's reply to Colonel Monro's appeal for a counterattack to break the siege. Webb offered no aid, except to suggest that Monro try to get the best surrender terms. Montcalm promptly forwarded the letter under a flag of truce; if anything could make the garrison see how foolish resistance had become, this was it.

Webb, paralyzed with fear, hid behind the walls of Fort Edward. Nothing could make him move, not even a tongue-lashing from Warraghiyagey. William Johnson, who'd been knighted for defeating Dieskau, arrived at Fort Edward with over a thousand colonials and Mohawks. He wanted to help.

"General Webb," he said sourly, "just what the hell are you doing sitting here when Fort William Henry is under attack? For God's sake, man, they need reinforcement and they need it *now!* Why isn't your army already on the move?"

"By what right," said Webb, rising from behind his desk, "do you come bursting into my office? Have you no conception, sir, of military courtesy?"

"Military courtesy, my foot!" Johnson snapped. "We've got men fighting and dying up at the lake. They have got to have help. *Now!*"

But Webb had already made up his mind to do nothing. "I can't send any. It would be useless with the few men I have. Suicide."

Sir William spoke softly, struggling to control his anger. He explained that the men he'd brought could easily attack the

French from behind. Montcalm didn't expect a counterattack, and, surely, he'd cave in at the first blow.

"Not so," said Webb.

That did it.

"By God," Johnson shouted, his face as red as his coat. "If *you* won't lead 'em, then let *me* do it. That same shore of Lake George can be just as fatal to Montcalm as it was for Dieskau. You give me the command, and I'll see French bones covering the battlefield!" With that, he whipped out his tomahawk and waved it in front of Webb's face. "By God, Webb, give your army to me, and I swear by my tomahawk that I'll conquer or die!"

"Don't you yell at me," cried the general. "I'm in command here—I'll make the decisions. I'll send no reinforcement to Fort William Henry."

Johnson was overcome with anger. He stood before Webb, legs apart, hands on hips, shaking with rage. Suddenly he tore the sleeves off his coat and flung them at the general's feet.

"You won't do it?" he bellowed.

"No."

He tore off buttons, coat, and shirt.

"You won't?"

"No."

Off came moccasins and pants until he stood stark naked. His Mohawks, meanwhile, had imitated Warraghiyagey's every move, so that Webb was surrounded by a mob of naked men holding guns and tomahawks.

By now, Johnson was so angry that words failed. He just stood there, glaring at Webb while his lips pursed and twitched. Then he coughed noisily and spit a mouthful of phlegm onto the general's desk, turned on his heel, and stormed out with his naked comrades.

Next day, August 9, 1757, the sixth day of the siege, a white flag fluttered above Fort William Henry. The surrender terms were generous. Montcalm didn't want prisoners, for there were already too many mouths to feed and food was scarce. Rather than hold the garrison, he promised to let them keep their weapons, although without ammunition or bayonets, and march to Fort Edward under escort. In exchange for freedom, they pledged not to serve against France for eighteen months.

Montcalm, however, knew that giving his word wasn't enough. The Indians had to agree; otherwise, they might turn the surrender into a massacre. Before signing the surrender document, he called the chiefs to a council to explain what he'd done and why. The chiefs agreed to everything and promised to control their braves. It was a meaningless promise, for nobody could control them if they decided otherwise.

The braves were disappointed and angry, all because of Montcalm's generosity. They had expected loot, and he was allowing the English to keep their possessions. They wanted scalps, and torture victims, and captives to adopt or hold for ransom; now Montcalm was setting his prisoners free. They'd fought hard and felt entitled to rewards for their efforts. If not, they'd take what was rightfully theirs, chiefs or no chiefs.

At noon French regulars escorted the garrison to the entrenched camp, where they'd spend the night before moving on to Fort Edward. Eighty-seven wounded and smallpox cases remained behind in the fort hospital. Since they were too ill to be moved, French surgeons were detailed to care for them.

No sooner had the garrison left the fort than a mob of Indians and *coureurs de bois* dashed through the open gate. They'd come for loot and, finding none, lost control. Howling with rage, they drew their tomahawks and scalping knives. All the wounded and sick were killed, along with several women and children who'd remained with their menfolk.

Father Roubaud, a French army chaplain, heard shrieks and ran to see what was the matter. He ran into a blood-spattered Abnaki. The brave had blood on his chin and at the corners of his mouth; he held by the hair the head of an Englishman. He held it high, gave a victory cry, and ran off with the trophy. Braves even dug up the smallpox cemetery to scalp the rotting corpses. It was only with difficulty that Montcalm's regulars cleared the fort with bayonets. Yet they came too late to save the helpless and the innocent.

The English spent a restless night in the entrenched camp. Montcalm had posted guards around the camp, but they were too few to keep out the Indians. Braves strutted about the encampment, pushing people aside and taking whatever they wanted from their baggage. Some pinched the cheeks and arms of men, while licking their lips and patting their stomachs. They also patted the long hair of women, often yanking it sharply. Things might have gotten out of hand had Montcalm not arrived to remind them of their chiefs' promises. He was still their great *Onontio,* and none dared defy him to his face. Unfortunately, he couldn't be everywhere at once.

At dawn, August 10, the English formed a column and began the fourteen-mile march to Fort Edward. Four hundred French regulars formed a rear and advance guard. The Indians, too, were wide awake.

As the column moved along the trail, painted braves crowded in on it from both sides. They began to jostle the fugitives and snatch their possessions away. Men were dragged from the column and the clothes stripped from their backs. There were screams as women and children were grabbed and hauled into the woods.

Braves were especially interested in the soldiers' canteens. They knew that the English had been ordered to get rid of their rum; they also thought that many would disobey the order. And they were right, for about half the canteens were filled with the strong liquor.

Frenzied braves danced and waved tomahawks as they poured rum down their throats. Suddenly, a tall Abnaki cupped his hands to his mouth and gave a bloodcurdling war cry. "*Eeeeeee-Neeeee-Yaaaahhhhhh!*"

Hundreds took up the cry and began killing the defenseless English. *Coureurs de bois* looked on, delighted, or encouraged their friends to hack away. Hysterical men begged Canadian officers on their knees for protection but were refused with shouts of "English dog!" The outnumbered regulars were powerless against the mob.

Montcalm heard the uproar and came running with his officers. This was not what he wanted, or expected, and he felt ashamed. He stood in the midst of the slaughter and tore open his shirt. "Kill me, but spare the English who are under my protection," he shouted, pointing to his bare chest. About a hundred English were already dead, but Montcalm put hundreds of others nearby under his personal protection. More regulars were called.

The rest of the English stampeded down the trail or stumbled through the woods, where they soon became lost. Many were naked, having been stripped by the Indians. Hundreds had deep cuts and large bruises covering their bodies. General Webb ordered signal guns fired every few minutes to guide them to Fort Edward. That was the full extent of the help he gave.

A week later, Indians brought two hundred prisoners to Montreal. They were a sorry-looking lot—bloody, starving, and with terror in their eyes. Governor Vaudreuil ransomed most of the captives with two kegs of brandy for each. Those who the Indians refused to ransom were saved for their victory celebration.

Bougainville, who had arrived the day before with Montcalm's report of the siege, was horrified at what he saw. The Indians got drunk and ran through the streets pushing, kicking, and threatening Canadians. Growing tired of this, they put on a "show" in the middle of the main street. "At two o'clock," Bougainville wrote his mother, "in the presence of the entire city, the

Indians killed one of the English soldiers, put him in a kettle, and forced his unfortunate comrades to eat him." Bougainville could only add, sadly, "What a land! What a people!"

Although Montcalm had risked his life to save prisoners, the massacre left a stain on an otherwise clean reputation. Englishmen never forgot, or forgave, what happened at Fort William Henry. Sooner or later, they vowed, they would pay off the murderers. If ever a French garrison fell into their power, the regulars would be treated as prisoners of war. It would be otherwise with Indians and Canadians, especially *coureurs de bois.*

The French army broke up immediately after Fort William Henry's garrison was freed. The fort was burned and the Canadians rushed back to their farms. Only the regulars remained, and they weren't enough to continue the campaign. Montcalm withdrew to Ticonderoga and then to Montreal to plan his next moves.

The Indians, too, went home. They brought loot, and scalps, and stories of their own heroism. Those who had scalped the dead in the smallpox cemetery brought something extra: smallpox germs. During the fall and winter of 1757, the disease raged among the tribes of the western Great Lakes and prairies. Tribesmen, delirious with fever, leaped into streams and drowned. People covered with tiny, puss-filled sores were driven mad by the itching and scratched themselves raw; many went blind. Nearly the entire Potawatomi nation perished. Thus, at least some of the fort's victims took their revenge.

AN UNEASY QUIET settled over the frontiers for nearly a year after Montcalm's victory. While garrison troops huddled behind log walls, Canadians and Indians played a vicious game of hide-and-seek in the woods between Crown Point and Fort Edward. Roving bands searched out victims and took those prisoners with useful information; the threat of "special treatment" by the Indians never failed to loosen a captive's tongue.

Yet these bands went in fear, for they knew that the enemy had caught on to their tricks; indeed, he invented some nasty tricks of his own. By 1757, ranging companies, officially known as "light infantry," had become part of the British army in America. Instead of wearing the regular's red coat, their dress uniform was forest green topped with a black cap and a large feather. When they fought, however, rangers wore buckskin and moccasins; the leather tassles dangling from their jackets were useful for everything from mending snowshoes to tourniquets to stop bleeding. They were every bit as tough as their comrades in frontier Virginia and Pennsylvania. And the toughest of all, Rogers's Rangers, were based at Fort Edward.

Major Robert Rogers, their commander, was a barrel-chested six-footer with the face of a boxer, complete with a nose that had come into contact with too many fists. Born in 1731, Rogers had grown up in backwoods New Hampshire. His boyhood memories were not of good times with friends, but of backbreaking farm work and Indian raids.

He gained from both experiences. The work made him hard and gave him endurance; he could run for hours with pack and musket without getting winded. The raids taught him that, to survive, you needed cunning as well as courage. Rogers fought hard, drank much, and had several brushes with the law; he was once accused of counterfeiting and was suspected of smuggling. But in the 1750s, his skills were in demand and no one looked into his past too carefully.

Rogers joined the rangers and soon formed a company of his own. Rogers's Rangers became the best unit of its kind in the British army. The major made a science of fighting and surviving in the forest. Woodcraft, tracking, camouflage, signaling, ambushing, and tomahawk throwing were basic skills. Volunteers mastered these skills or they washed out of the outfit. Today's

LE MAJOR ROBERT ROGER
Commandant en Chef les Troupes Indiennes au service des
Américains

*Major Robert Rogers of the Rangers in dress uniform. Rogers was a master
of forest warfare, copying and improving upon Indian methods of tracking
and surprise attack. From a 1776 engraving.*

Green Berets and British commandos follow in the footsteps of these eighteenth-century woodsmen.

Rogers's Rangers fought anywhere, anytime. During the warm months, they portaged canoes to Lake George and Lake Champlain. Hiding by day and traveling by night, but only when clouds hid the moon, they scouted the area around the French forts. In winter, they crossed spotless snowfields on snowshoes or skated in darkness past the forts on the frozen surface of Lake Champlain.

Rogers had the gift of putting himself into the enemy's mind and thinking his thoughts. Then he did the opposite, striking swiftly where least expected. Indians called him "the White Devil," and he lived up to the name.

The rangers walked Indian file, ten feet apart, in complete silence. Not a twig snapped, or a branch creaked, as they passed. Pointmen, rear guard, and flankers were always on the alert to danger. One of Rogers's officers had a great furry beast, half wolf and half dog, that could sniff out any Indian. When the enemy was sighted, Rogers gave a hand signal—"Tree all!"—and his men faded into the underbrush. For safety, each ranger was paired with a partner. Partners never fired at once, since that would have allowed the enemy to rush them while reloading. One fired, and, as he reloaded, his partner covered him. If the fighting became too hot, the Rangers scattered and reassembled at a prearranged spot miles from the battleground.

Rogers specialized in ambushing war parties and taking prisoners for questioning. Wounded captives unable to travel had to be killed to prevent discovery. They were, he explained calmly, "knock'd on the head."

Rogers became so bold that he struck within a few hundred yards of Fort Carillon. Once he butchered fifteen head of cattle to feed his men and, to be polite, left a note for the French commander: "I am obliged to you, sir, for . . . the fresh meat you have sent me. I shall take good care of my prisoners. My compliments to the Marquis of Montcalm." Signed, Rogers. The French weren't amused and swore revenge. Their chance came in March 1758, during the Battle of the Snowshoes.

It began as a routine mission to the Ticonderoga area. Rogers left Fort Edward with 180 officers and men, who looked more like tramps than soldiers. Each wore snowshoes and carried a food knapsack slung over his left shoulder, along with a powder horn and bullet pouch; a canteen filled with rum dangled under the right shoulder. Blankets were passed over their heads like monks' hoods and fastened with a belt around the waist. Mittens were tied to the blanket with cords.

The temperature dropped to ten degrees below zero and wind gusts stung their eyes, already watering from the reflections of sun on snow. Cautiously, the party slipped through the frozen wilderness. Arriving at Lake George, it crossed on ice creepers, saw-toothed devices attached to the feet to give traction on slippery surfaces. All was quiet, all went well—*too* well.

They had gone several miles up the lake when Rogers had a crawly feeling at the back of the neck, as if he sensed eyes following him from the shoreline. His instinct was correct, although he chose to ignore the warning. That was a mistake that would cost many lives.

The French had brought in Langy de Montegron, master of the ambush, to deal with the rangers. Montegron decided to go "fishing," that is, to set out ambush bait and, when Rogers snapped at it, pull him in.

Rogers came to a valley behind a bald-faced mountain near the northern end of Lake George. A stream flowed through the valley; it was frozen now, forming a pathway through the tangled brush and snowdrifts on either bank. Here, he thought, was the perfect place to set a trap. He was right.

Scouts rushed back with news that a hundred Indians were coming along the frozen stream. Rogers gave the "Tree all!"

signal and within seconds only windblown snowflakes could be seen bouncing across the ice.

As expected, the enemy soon appeared, painted braves with blankets draped over their heads and shoulders. As planned, Rogers's Rangers cut down more than half of them at the first volley. The survivors turned tail and ran, pursued by about ninety Rangers.

Suddenly, the crash of gunfire and war whoops came from up ahead. Rogers's men had run smack into Montegron's main body—four hundred Canadians and Indians. The rangers never had a chance.

During the next three hours, the remaining rangers were pushed steadily up the mountainside. Darting from rock to rock, tree to tree, they paused only to reload and fire again. But they were outnumbered four to one. Their only hope was that darkness would come before their ammunition ran out or the enemy slipped behind them.

Toward sunset, a detachment under Lieutenant Phillips was surrounded and forced to surrender. Despite Montegron's promise of kind treatment, they were tied to trees and hacked to bits.

Their comrades—the lucky ones—escaped as best they could. It was every man for himself. Rogers took off his coat and slid to safety at a place still known as "Rogers's Slide." When the French found the coat, they assumed that they were finally rid of the New Hampshire daredevil. "Rogers is killed completely, coat, and breeches!" said the official report. They'd soon learn otherwise.

In the meantime, he'd suffered a terrible defeat. Only fifty-four men, including their commander, returned to Fort Edward. Yet Robert Rogers had a way of recovering from setbacks. Within two months, he was back in the woods with a fresh group of rangers. Never again would he fall for ambush bait.

THE ENGLISH were getting used to bad news. Except for Johnson's victory over Dieskau, nothing had gone well for them since the war began. In Europe, as in America, they had suffered one disaster after another. Their island base of Minorca in the Mediterranean Sea was captured and John Byng, the admiral charged with its loss, executed for incompetence. King Frederick the Great of Prussia, England's ally among the German states, was fighting for his life against the combined forces of Austria, Russia, and France. If Frederick went under, defeat for England was a certainty.

Just when things looked blackest, in December 1756, a new prime minister took office. Born in 1708, William Pitt, earl of Chatham, was a nervous, melancholy man who, friends feared, might commit suicide. They were wrong. For although Pitt occasionally broke down from overwork, weeping uncontrollably, he had a will of iron. Once he decided to do something, he allowed nothing to stand in his path. In his own way, William Pitt was a hero.

Like King William III, he vowed to defeat France, regardless of cost or sacrifice. Pitt enlarged the army and promoted talented young officers over the heads of the seniors. Money was no object when it came to the war effort. He raised taxes and borrowed huge sums from the British people. He spent so freely that people said he "broke windows with guineas"—gold coins worth about five hundred dollars in today's money.

Pitt changed the pattern set during the earlier French wars. He concentrated on America, not Europe, for he believed that Britain's future lay in building a vast empire overseas. Thus, Frederick the Great received all the money he needed to tie down France in Europe, freeing Britain for the war at sea and in North America.

Prime Minister William Pitt drew up plans to concentrate British forces in the colonies, leaving Prussia and other allies to deal with France in Europe.

Pitt's master plan called for redcoats and colonial militia to join forces to destroy New France within three years. Over 25,000 regulars were sent across the Atlantic, while an equal number of militia was to be raised in the colonies. The king would pay all costs or repay the colonies for their expenses. Their objectives for 1758 were the three fortresses guarding the approaches to Canada: the Lake Champlain forts, Fort Duquesne, Louisbourg. Quebec, stripped of its outer defenses, would be taken the following year.

THE LAKE CHAMPLAIN FORTS were to be captured by General James Abercromby, known to his men as "Aunt Abby" and "Mrs. Nabbycrumby." An army old-timer, he was slow moving, bumbling, and, if we believe his brother officers, a fool. But he was a fool with friends, among them King George II, who saw to it that he won command of the forces in America.

Pitt still felt confident, for Aunt Abby always took the advice of his second-in-command, a military genius and the most popular officer in the British army. Brigadier General George Augustus, Lord Howe, was a nobleman and a member of the royal family. Handsome, brave, and a natural leader, Howe knew how to inspire confidence in men of all ranks. At a time when officers treated common soldiers as ignorant brutes, Howe made them feel needed and trusted. Howe often visited the troops at their watch fires and helped himself to meat from the mess pot with a large clasp knife. He squatted next to them on stream banks to wash his own laundry. He was the only high-ranking officer to go on patrols with Rogers's Rangers. Soldiers loved Howe and would have followed him to the ends of the earth. Aunt Abby was lost without him.

Early in July 1758, the army assembled at the Great Carrying Place and moved overland to Lake George. Nothing like it had ever been seen in America; even Braddock's force was tiny by comparison. There were about 15,000 troops, redcoats and militia from New England, New York, and New Jersey. Rogers's Rangers and light infantry units came along as scouts, as did several hundred Mohawk under Sir William Johnson.

The Indians stared open-mouthed as the Black Watch, a regiment from the Scottish Highlands, came into camp. It marched to the skirl of bagpipes and the beating of drums. Each man wore a woolen kilt woven in stripes of black, blue, and green. He carried at his side a claymore, a double-edged sword with a blade as wide as his palm. One blow with a claymore could easily lop off an arm—or a head.

The army set out on Lake George on July 5. It was a glorious summer's day, warm and fresh, with not a cloud in the sky. A gentle breeze brought the scent of earth and trees from the surrounding hillsides. Swarms of ducks quacked and took flight as the British boats—over a thousand of them, plus artillery rafts— glided past their feeding sites. The procession of boats stretched from shore to shore and made a line six miles long. The men aboard felt invincible.

Reaching the upper end of the lake, they landed to make camp for the night. Next morning, Lord Howe joined Rogers's Rangers to scout the surrounding woods, where they blundered into a French patrol, which they easily wiped out. It was a small victory purchased at a high price. For when the smoke cleared, Lord Howe was found with a bullet through the heart.

His death came as a blow to the army. "In Lord Howe," wrote Major Thomas Mante, a brother officer, "the soul of General Abercromby's army seemed to expire. From the unhappy moment the general was deprived of his advice, neither order nor discipline was observed. . . ." Despite their numbers, the men began to think that the expedition was cursed. Abercromby became confused; his mind seemed to go blank. As a result, he spent the next day, July 7, fussing and fretting in camp. That lost day allowed Montcalm to make his preparations.

Montcalm had arrived at Fort Carillon with fresh troops a few days earlier. He saw immediately that he couldn't wait for the

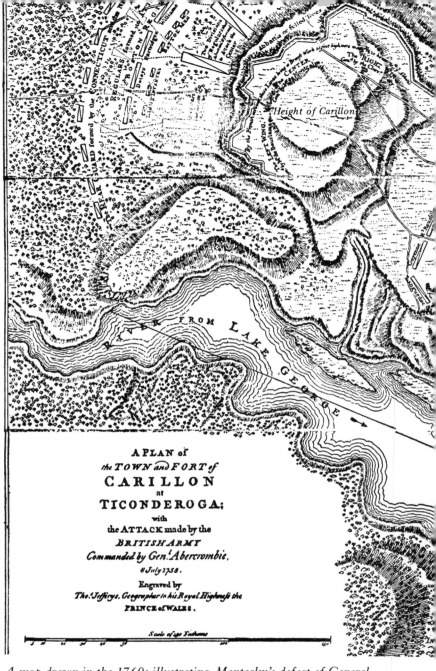

A map drawn in the 1760s illustrating Montcalm's defeat of General
Abercromby outside Fort Carillon on the Ticonderoga peninsula. Notice the
star-shaped design of the fort, used to catch the enemy in a crossfire between

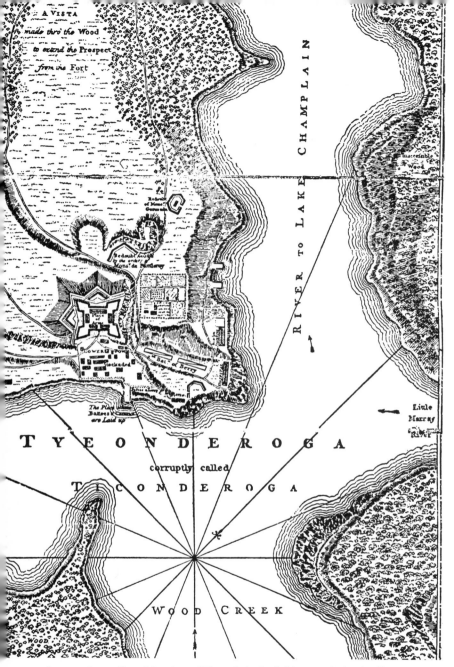

A VISTA
made thro' the Wood
to extend the Prospect
from the Fort

RIVER TO LAKE CHAMPLAIN

Redoubt
of Mons
Germa

Redoubt raised
by the orders
Mons. de Montcalm

Inaccessible
Wood

LOWER FORT
Stockade

Barbet Battery

The Place
Battoes & Cannon
are Laid up

Little
Harray
River

T Y E O N D E R O G A

corruptly called

T I C O N D E R O G A

W O O D   C R E E K

WOOD

the curtain wall and bastions. The original of this map is in the Fort Ticonderoga Museum.

British to attack him in the fort. His 3500 regulars were too large a force to remain in the fort and too small to fight European-style in the open. Worse, his provisions would last five days at the most. To win, he must bring Abercromby to battle outside the fort and pray that his foe would do something stupid. If not, Montcalm knew that he was lost.

Fort Carillon lay at the end of the Ticonderoga peninsula, a wedge-shaped piece of land surrounded by water on three sides. About a mile from the fort, a narrow ridge rises across the neck of the peninsula and falls sharply to the shore on the other side. Here the French prepared to fight their battle.

Montcalm set his troops to work with pick, ax, and shovel. Thousands of trees were cut down in front of the position to give a clear field of fire. Logs were then arranged in a zigzagging barricade eight feet high and topped with sandbags; the zigzag design, like a fort's bastions, made it possible to catch attackers in a crossfire at every angle. The barricade was loopholed so that the defenders could fire without exposing themselves.

A zigzagging ditch was dug in front of the barricade, which was protected in turn by an abatis fifty feet wide. A Roman invention, the abatis is a barrier of felled trees with their branches sharpened and pointing toward the attacker. The barbed-wire entanglements of modern wars work on the same principle.

Montcalm's defense line was still incomplete, but good enough, when a signal gun sounded from the walls of Fort Carillon. The British were coming.

Abercromby had everything in his favor: numbers, artillery, provisions, time. If he had wanted to be cautious, he could have blockaded the peninsula and waited for starvation to force a surrender. If he had chosen to get it over with quickly, he could have let the artillery blast the barricade to splinters. He did neither, choosing instead the worst possible plan. To this day, no one can say why he acted so foolishly. Perhaps Lord Howe's death made him temporarily insane.

Rather than study the French position for himself, Abercromby sent an inexperienced young engineering officer to tell him what was happening. The officer reported that there was no need for artillery. The defenses were so weak, he said, that they could easily be taken by head-on infantry assault. The big guns should remain on their rafts offshore.

Montcalm's men stood three deep behind their barricade. Those in front peered through the loopholes, anxious for a glimpse of the enemy. Soon rangers were seen scurrying through the woods to the right and left of the clearing. Within minutes, every tree and stump concealed a rifleman. Johnson and his Mohawks sat atop Defiance Mountain; they watched the whole battle from their post without firing a shot.

After a while, masses of red began to show through the trees. Abercromby's main force stepped into the clearing and began to advance in four massive columns. Officers with swords resting across the right shoulder marched in front and beside each column. Sergeants bawled commands to step lively, straighten the line, and look smart. "Remember," they cried, "no firing at all. Nothing but the bayonet; and follow the officers in."

The French sucked in their breath. Montcalm, at the center of the barricade, drew his sword. His officers watched him, ready to relay his orders in an instant. "Steady," he cautioned. "Hold your fire until I give the signal."

The British columns rolled forward like a crimson tide, muskets shouldered and bayonets gleaming. Drummers measured the pace with a steady *tap, tap, tap.*

A quarter mile from the barricade, the leading officers waved their swords. The harsh notes of bugles echoed across the hills.

Charge!

The redcoats gripped their muskets with both hands, bayonets pointing ahead, and began to run. "God save the king!" they roared. To cover them, the rangers opened fire on the loopholes across the way.

Montcalm raised his sword. A sharp *click* rippled down the line as 3500 hands cocked thirty-five hundred muskets. The veterans of Fort William Henry would have given anything to have their Indian allies today; unfortunately, there hadn't been time to send the red hatchet among the tribes. They'd have to do this job themselves.

Montcalm brought his sword down with a swift, slashing motion. Instantly his officers did the same.

"*Fire!*"

A sheet of flame swept from the zigzag wall and mowed down the ranks of the oncoming columns. But no sooner did a man topple than another stepped over the body to fill the gap in the ranks. They kept coming without missing a step.

"*Fire!*"

Again a sheet of flame. Again more bodies. Redcoats fell by the score, by entire companies, but their sacrifice meant nothing. A handful reached the abatis, only to be shot as they became tangled in the branches. At last the column halted, paused for a moment, then retreated to the safety of the tree line. From behind they heard cries of "*Vive le roi!*" and "*Vive notre général!*" "Long live the king! Long live our general!"

Aunt Abby remained at his headquarters, an abandoned sawmill near the lake. Not once did he bother to see the results of his orders with his own eyes.

The woods around his headquarters became choked with moaning, mangled men. Surgeons worked with rolled-up sleeves; their canvas smocks, like butchers' aprons, were spattered with blood. The general saw none of this, nor did he care to see. His only contribution was to order a new attack after learning that the last one had failed. Six times the British charged, and six times they were hurled back with heavy losses in dead and wounded.

The Black Watch led the last attack. With swinging kilts and skirling bagpipes, they marched into the enemy's line of fire. Suddenly they tossed away their muskets, drew their claymores,

"Aunt Abby" Abercromby tried to overwhelm Montcalm's barricade at Ticonderoga with manpower instead of using the artillery he'd brought along on his expedition to Lake Champlain. Despite their courage, the Redcoats and Highlanders failed to dent the French position.

and began hacking at the abatis in frustration. One half the regiment—499 men—fell in just a few minutes.

The sun was setting when Aunt Abby ordered a retreat to Fort Edward. He had lost about 2000 men—killed, wounded, and missing. Most of his cannon had been abandoned without having fired a shot. The fighting had cost Montcalm fewer than 400 casualties.

The French were overjoyed. They'd won again, this time against odds of better than four to one. In gratitude to God, they raised a giant wooden cross on the battlefield and knelt before it in prayer. A replica of that cross stands on the same spot today.

Although they couldn't know it then, there'd be no more thanksgivings for victory. For eighteen days later, the tide of war turned against the French. On July 26, 1758, Louisbourg fell for the second time, dooming New France.

⸙ V ⸙

To the Plains
of Abraham

TOWARD MIDNIGHT, June 1, 1758, lookouts on Cape Breton Island noticed something odd. Fog had shrouded the island for weeks, but now it cleared just enough to show lights flickering in the blackness offshore. Dawn revealed a vast fleet lying outside Gabarus Bay six miles west of Louisbourg. At their mastheads the ships flew the white ensign, a white banner with a red cross, the colors of Britain's Royal Navy.

The fleet had sailed from Halifax, Nova Scotia, the previous day. Nothing had been done to conceal its movements, for it feared nothing in American waters. It consisted of thirty-nine warships escorting one hundred and ten transports, storage vessels, and supply ships. Half the warships were "ships-of-the-line," ancestors of the modern battleship. These floating castles mounted as many as a hundred cannons on three gun decks. Slow moving and hard-to-handle, they could deliver a crushing salvo at close range. Smaller vessels called "frigates" were faster and handled more easily, although they lacked the ships-of-the-line's firepower.

The fleet carried the flower of Great Britain's armed forces. Twelve thousand sailors and marines manned the ships; ten thousand soldiers were crowded aboard the transports. Redcoats formed the army's backbone, supported by Highlanders, light infantry, rangers, and about 500 colonial militia.

The expedition's commanders were Prime Minister Pitt's own choices, not royal favorites. The commander–in–chief was Major General Jeffrey Amherst, a career officer with plenty of battlefield experience in Europe. Amherst at forty-one was a tall, ramrod-straight man with red hair, red eyebrows, and a red face. Though brave, he wasn't reckless. Calm and thoughtful, he never left anything to chance. He personally planned everything, thought of everything, saw that everything went smoothly. Lives and time were precious to him, and he wasted neither.

Amherst's naval commander was Vice Admiral Edward Boscawen. This crusty saltwater sailor had spent practically all of his forty-eight years at sea. Crewmen called him "Old Dreadnought," a name he well deserved. Boscawen was fearless and would fight anyone or anything afloat. One night in the English Channel, an officer awakened him to report two large French men-of-war bearing down under full sail. "What shall we do, sir?" the officer asked. "*Do,* sir?" the admiral shouted, pulling on his breeches. "*Do?* Why, damn 'em, fight 'em, of course!" So fight they did, and won. No wonder Great Britain's first modern battleships were called "dreadnoughts"; like their namesake, they dreaded nothing at sea.

Amherst's field commander, who'd do the actual fighting ashore, had recently been promoted from colonel to brigadier general. Although unknown outside the army, thirty-one-year-old James Wolfe would soon become a national hero. Wolfe stood six feet three inches tall, was thin as a broomstick, and had orange-red hair with a complexion the color of library paste. He described himself as "a skeleton in motion" and lived every day of his life in intense pain. He suffered from tuberculosis, kidney disease, rheumatism, fevers, dizziness, and an unnamed disease he believed was slowly killing him. He took scores of medicines, mostly disgusting, including one made almost entirely of soap. As a boy, his mother had treated him with a syrup made of crushed garden snails, green earthworms, bear's foot, powdered deer bone, and roots. Brother officers thought him the most unsoldierly soldier they'd ever known. He never gambled or got drunk, but spent his spare time reading poetry.

Yet this wreck of a man had the heart of a lion. Like Montcalm, he was born to be a soldier. The Wolfes had been soldiers for centuries; his father, Edward, was a colonel of marines who had fought Frenchmen for fifty years. James joined the army at fifteen and dedicated himself to becoming the best soldier possible. He read every book on the art of war, ancient and modern, in English, French, and Latin. His quick mind and ready courage won him repeated promotion.

Troops respected "Jaimie" Wolfe and counted him a friend; they even sang a song—"Hot Stuff"—about his adventures. There were two ways of doing things: Wolfe's and the army rule book's. Wolfe preferred his own methods and kept to them. He had his regiment's uniforms cut more comfortably and outlawed whipping. Soldiers were men, not beasts, and he insisted upon humane discipline. When some officers apologized for not teaching their companies certain new exercises, he replied, "Poh, poh! New exercises, new fiddlesticks. If they are otherwise well disciplined and will fight, that's all I require of them." That's really all he required of himself, too. For James Wolfe's highest ambition was to die gallantly in battle against his country's foes.

The British commanders expected a hard fight for Louisbourg. After the fortress's return to France in 1748, its defenses had been repaired and strengthened. The Chevalier de Drucour, its governor, was an experienced professional skilled in fortress warfare. His troops numbered thirty-one hundred regulars, plus a thousand Canadians and five hundred Indians. The citadel

Lord Jeffrey Amherst, commander in chief of the British armies in North America, 1758–1763. Amherst was a cautious soldier who preferred to "waste" time making good plans rather than lose men's lives through haste or carelessness.

"Old Dreadnought," Admiral Edward Boscawen, led the British fleet at Louisbourg in 1758.

mounted two hundred and thirty-seven guns on its walls, not to mention those in the Grand and Island batteries and a new battery at Lighthouse Point. There were also ten warships in the harbor, ships-of-the-line and frigates, with over five hundred guns and three thousand seamen. Drucour had cannons zeroed in on likely landing sites. Trenches topped with sandbags overlooked the beaches from the cliffs.

Louisbourg's defenders were ready and eager to meet any invaders. But no sooner did Amherst's fleet appear than it vanished. Fog rolled in again, and storms, blotting out the coastline. Each morning, ashen-faced soldiers peered into the grayness; the only sign of land was the roar of breakers crashing against invisible rocks. Had it not been for the skill of Boscawen's captains, the fleet might have run aground. Finally, the fog lifted and at dawn, June 8, 1758, Amherst gave the attack order.

The landing at Louisbourg was to become a model for future amphibious operations. Both services cooperated fully toward their common goal. Bugles alerted the troops; pennants hoisted on the masthead of *Namur,* Boscawen's flagship, relayed instructions to the ship captains. Slowly, the warships lined up broadside to the citadel and the shore batteries. Troops climbed down rope ladders hung over the transports' sides and into the waiting longboats. When each longboat was filled, sailors cast off and rowed to their assigned jump-off points.

The longboats were arranged in three divisions—red, blue, white—each under its own commander. But only Wolfe's division, the red, would try for a landing. The others were decoys to lure the French away from the true landing site. Once Wolfe secured a beachhead, they would come in as the second and third waves. Their orders were to land quickly and clear off the beach to allow the artillery to be brought ashore.

The longboats had gone only a few hundred yards when the warships opened fire. The boom of cannon rolled across the water to the crowded boats. The men heard the roar and felt the vibrations in their guts. Drifting gunsmoke stung their eyes. Occasionally, "shorts"—cannonballs that fell short of their targets—sent fountains of water leaping skyward, then cascading down upon the redcoats.

Twelve hundred Frenchmen watched Wolfe's approach from their trenches. They could see the sailors' pigtails and hear the soldiers calling to each other from their boats. The French held their fire until the last possible moment, then opened up with everything they had.

Boats flew apart in showers of splinters. Boats overturned, dumping men into the sea, to be dragged under by their backpacks and waterlogged uniforms. Sailors pulling at oars were shot in the back, as were many who tried to toss a rope to a drowning redcoat.

Wolfe's heart sank as weeks of planning were being shot to pieces before his eyes. He was waving his cane to signal retreat when he noticed three boats on his right speed toward a rocky shelf jutting from the shore, the entrance to a half-hidden cove. Within seconds, the boats vanished behind the rocks.

That was all Wolfe needed. Standing in the bow of his boat, he waved his cane furiously and shouted for the others to follow. It was a wild, wet ride. Boats skidded across the foamy water, heading for the white line of waves breaking against the shore. Wind whistled. Men were drenched with salt spray. Many boats overturned or splintered on the rocks. Many men drowned. But their comrades, sputtering and spitting, their weapons and powder flasks soaked, stumbled through the surf.

"Who were the first ashore?" Wolfe asked as they formed into squads.

Two men were pointed out.

"Good fellows!" he said, smiling, and gave each a golden guinea, worth a half-year's pay.

Wolfe's men were angrier than wet cats. They'd taken a lot, and now wanted to repay "Frenchie" in his own coin. But since

General James Wolfe was tall, thin, and usually in poor health. The black cloth worn around his left arm in this portrait by H. Smyth is in mourning for his father, who died shortly before the attack on Louisbourg.

their muskets were useless, they fixed bayonets; the Highlanders drew their claymores. The French, startled at their determination, scrambled out of their trenches and ran for safety in Louisbourg. The invaders had won the first round.

With a beachhead secured, the artillery was landed by evening. As in 1745, the heavy pieces had to be hauled across the marshes between the beach and the low hills behind the citadel. Army engineers promptly began to survey a road. It took longer to build than the Yankees' stone boats, but the result was a permanent highway. The British were also building for the future; this time they meant to keep Cape Breton Island and would need the road for their own garrison.

Women as well as men helped haul the guns. Several hundred women had joined the fleet as laundresses and cooks, and they volunteered to harness themselves to the drag ropes. They pulled away, never flinching even when the French lobbed shells at them from the citadel. Once the guns were emplaced, women helped the crews with loading and firing.

Within a week, Wolfe had surrounded the citadel with a ring of iron. But before the ring closed, Governor Drucour abandoned his outlying fortifications for lack of manpower to hold them. One night, the guns of the Grand Battery and Lighthouse Point were removed to the citadel. Whatever couldn't be salvaged was destroyed.

The siege now began to move like clockwork. Wolfe occupied the abandoned positions and set up his own guns, big forty-two pounders. Soon the Island Battery, harbor, and eastern walls of Louisbourg were being raked by gunfire.

The French fought back bravely. Each morning, regardless of danger, Madame Drucour mounted the walls to begin the day's fighting by firing three cannon with her own hands. Amherst admired her courage and sent her some pineapples as a gift. She and her husband returned the courtesy with fifty bottles of champagne.

Despite these niceties, the siege continued with growing fury. Louisbourg echoed to the sound of crumbling buildings and the cries of wounded men and animals. The air seemed always to be filled with cinders and smoke; even food tasted gritty and burned. Hot shot—cannonballs heated in a furnace before being rolled down a gun barrel—set the hospital on fire. An exploding shell fell into the barracks, destroying them. From then on, the troops had to sleep in the streets, alongside sailors who'd been ordered ashore to man the fortifications. Louisbourg was dying. An officer wrote in his diary: "Not a house in the whole place but has felt the force of their cannonade. Between yesterday morning and seven o'clock tonight from a thousand to twelve hundred shells have fallen inside the town. . . . The surgeons have to run at many a cry of '*Ware shell!* for fear lest they should share their patients' fate."

The warships in the harbor were useless. With only skeleton crews, and most of their guns removed to the citadel, they rode at anchor near the town. One night, an unknown Englishman (or woman) got lucky—really lucky. The gunner put an exploding shell squarely on the deck of *Célèbre,* the man-of-war nearest the town. The shell went off in a pile of gunpowder barrels, blowing the vessel sky-high. Flaming wreckage ignited the sails of her neighbor, *Entreprenant.* Burning bits of canvas then drifted over to *Capricieux.* Louisbourg harbor lit up in an eerie, wavering, orange light. *Entreprenant* and *Capricieux* stood outlined in fire against the black sky. Their tarred ropes burned, resembling enormous spiderwebs. Nothing remained by sunrise except hissing timbers.

The final blow fell on the night of July 25. At midnight, Old Dreadnought sent twenty-five boatloads of marines into the harbor. Silently, rowing with muffled oars, they split into two units and made for their objectives, the two largest of the remaining French warships. Nearing the *Prudent,* they were challenged by the watch, a lone sentry. A voice called out in perfect French,

A view of Louisbourg when that city was besieged in 1758 by Lord Amherst's fleet.

explaining that the boats were bringing a relief crew. But no sooner did they bump against the *Prudent*'s side than barefooted Englishmen leaped over the deck rail with swords and pistols. The skeleton crew was captured in their hammocks without having fired a shot. Unfortunately, the *Prudent* was aground on a sandbar and had to be burned.

The second unit had better luck with the *Bienfaisant*. While some boarders held her crew at gunpoint, others threw lines to the longboats and towed her away. As she glided past Lighthouse Point, redcoats cheered themselves hoarse.

That was the last straw. Next morning, Drucour asked for surrender terms. They were not generous. Amherst promised the French regulars their lives, but no honors of war. No terms were offered to Canadians or Indians; if captured, they would be

treated the same as the garrison of Fort William Henry. That
night, as the redcoats prepared to occupy the town, the Canadians
and Indians paddled away in their canoes. The French troops
were sent to England as prisoners of war, where they remained
for five miserable years. Their families and the people of Louisbourg were deported to France, where they received a cold welcome; many died in poverty.

The invasion force broke up within weeks of its victory.
Several regiments remained behind to garrison their prize. Boscawen put to sea with the fleet to hunt Frenchmen. Wolfe sailed
back to England to await further orders. Amherst took most of

OVERLEAF:
Capture of the Bienfaisant *at Louisbourg, July 26, 1758, while her sister
ship, the* Prudent, *burns.*

the troops to New York to clean up the mess left by Aunt Abby, who had been forced to retire from the service.

News of Louisbourg's fall was the first bright spot in four years of fighting. The British colonies went wild with joy. Balls and fireworks, parades and thanksgiving services, were held throughout the land. In England, Parliament passed votes of thanks to Amherst and his commanders. Jaimie Wolfe's name was on everyone's lips. He'd already been marked for a special assignment by Prime Minister Pitt.

The French received the news more soberly. "Woe to this land!" wrote Bougainville in his diary a few days after the surrender. He knew, as Montcalm knew, that the enemy now held the key to the St. Lawrence in his hands.

As for Louisbourg itself, Pitt ordered it destroyed two years later. Today, nothing remains of the fortress and town except some overgrown fragments of wall. And, it's been said, the ghosts of soldiers long dead.

THE ENGLISH chose their next targets carefully. As Wolfe's guns pounded Louisbourg, Lieutenant Colonel John Bradstreet led three thousand men, regulars and colonials, to the Mohawk River near Schenectady. There they loaded supplies, including heavy cannon, and boarded bateaux for the westward journey. They moved easily because, after the fall of Oswego, the French believed the enemy had abandoned "the Bloody Mohawk."

Bradstreet's objective was Fort Frontenac. Located where Lake Ontario joins the St. Lawrence, Fort Frontenac was chief supply base for French outposts on the Great Lakes and along the Ohio River. Its warehouses brimmed with munitions, clothing, and food for the coming winter. Trade goods to buy Indian furs, and gifts to keep their loyalty, stood in great mounds ready for shipment.

For such an important place, Fort Frontenac was badly un-dermanned. Its 110-man garrison was in no way able to withstand a siege with artillery. The fort was in such poor condition that, an officer complained, it shook whenever a cannon was fired from the walls.

Bradstreet made his final preparations at the ruins of the Oswego forts. When all was ready, he set out across Lake Ontario. The rest was easy. On August 27, 1758, Fort Frontenac surrendered after a brief bombardment. Bradstreet's men could hardly believe their eyes when they broke into the warehouses. In addition to seventy-six dismounted cannon, they found ten thousand barrels of food, trade goods, and bales of furs. Everything was burned.

The loss of these supplies was soon felt throughout the French West. On the Ohio, the men of Fort Duquesne tightened their belts and settled down to a winter on quarter-rations. Governor Vaudreuil sent orders to retreat upriver if the enemy appeared.

Throughout the fall, the British had been preparing to settle scores with Fort Duquesne. Brigadier General John Forbes had assembled five thousand colonials and fifteen hundred Highlanders at Fort Cumberland, Virginia, to do the job. Forbes, a dying man with only months to live, was so weak that he had to be carried in a litter slung between two horses. Yet his mind was sharp, and he had two assistants able to carry out his plans or act on their own when necessary. Lieutenant Colonel Henry Bouquet, his second-in-command, was a Swiss mercenary, a professional soldier who served the British for a price. He would soon be recognized as one of the finest Indian fighters in America. Colonel George Washington led the Virginia regiment. On this, his third visit to the Ohio country, he hoped to see the end of the French fort.

Forbes had learned the lessons of Braddock's Defeat. Instead of plunging headlong into the wilderness, he moved carefully, in measured stages. He struck northward from Fort Cumberland into Pennsylvania, then westward across the Alleghenies. The Pennsylvania route was longer than Braddock's, but easier and with more places to get fresh horses along the way. As the army advanced, blockhouses were built every few miles as strongpoints and supply depots. Such bases allowed the army to leapfrog ahead or fall back to prepared positions. Forbes was also generous with gifts to the local tribes.

Things went smoothly until Forbes sent Major James Grant ahead of the main force. Grant was to take eight hundred men, half Virginians and half Highlanders, to scout near Fort Duquesne and bring in prisoners for questioning. He must not—repeat, *not*—attack under any circumstances.

Grant, unfortunately, had other ideas. A mile from the fort, he split his detachment into thirds and advanced with bagpipes skirling, as if he meant to take the place on his own. Frenchmen and Indians swarmed out of the gate and cut off the Highlanders, many of whom failed to return to camp.

During the night of November 24, 1758, Forbes camped near Braddock's old battleground. Memories, and fears, crowded in upon the men as they settled down for a few hours' rest. Suddenly, a distant explosion shook the ground and a flash lit the sky. No one slept well that night.

Next morning, an advance party found the smoking ruins of Fort Duquesne; the French had blown it up and retreated upriver to Fort Venango. Amid the ruins, the British found Indian trophies—a double row of posts, each crowned with the head of a Highlander and a kilt tied beneath. Forbes ordered the remains buried and work begun on another fort, one so large that the whole of Fort Duquesne could have fit into its parade ground with room to spare. With the sounds of saws and hammers echoing in his ears, he wrote his report to William Pitt. He closed by telling the prime minister that he'd named the fort "Pitts-Borough" in his honor. We call it Pittsburgh.

IN LONDON, meanwhile, Pitt was putting the final touches to plans for destroying New France. Two armies were to close in, like the jaws of a giant nutcracker. Jeffrey Amherst was to advance up the Hudson Valley and, after capturing the Lake Champlain forts, invade Canada from the south. If all went well, he'd link up near Montreal with a second army driving along the St. Lawrence from Quebec.

Pitt had promoted Wolfe to major general and named him to lead the expedition against Quebec. But senior officers, jealous that one so young should hold such high rank, opposed the appointment. They began to whisper behind Wolfe's back and spread rumors that he was insane.

King George II thought the rumors nonsense and said so. "Mad is he?" snapped the king, remembering the years of defeat in America. "Then I hope he'll bite some of my other generals." Wolfe was the man for the job. There was nothing else to discuss or to whisper about. His Majesty had spoken.

Wolfe commanded the largest British force ever to cross the Atlantic. There were forty-nine men-of-war, one-quarter of the entire Royal Navy, plus two hundred transports, storage vessels, and provision ships. The fleet was so large that three admirals—Saunders, Holmes, Durrell—were needed to keep things in order. Its chief navigator was Captain James Cook, the future explorer of the Pacific. Nearly nine thousand redcoats and Highlanders were carried in the transports.

After stopovers at Halifax and Louisbourg to pick up several hundred colonial rangers, the fleet sailed for the St. Lawrence in mid-June 1759. Rounding the Gaspé Peninsula, it entered the mouth of the mighty river. Dense forests lined the bluffs for hundreds of miles, silent except when a flight of honking geese soared out across the water. Redcoated officers clinked glasses in a toast: "British colors on every French fort, post, and garrison in America."

Men grew serious as the fleet neared the Isle aux Coudres forty miles below Quebec. The river narrows here, becoming swifter and treacherous. Shallows, sandbars, and submerged rocks lie in wait for the unwary mariner. The French feared the place and stationed pilots on the island to guide ships through the channel. Even so, since Champlain's day they never passed more than one ship up the channel at a time, and this was usually no more than a few hundred tons. They thought it madness to attempt to sail thousand-ton men-of-war, let alone an entire battle fleet, past the Isle aux Coudres.

One day, lookouts at the pilot station on the island saw several ships appear. At their mastheads they flew the colors of France, golden lilies on a field of white. Without pausing for a closer look, the excited men paddled out to greet them. But no sooner did they climb onto the deck of the leading vessel than their smiles turned to scowls. For staring them in the eye were mean-looking sailors with swords. As they motioned the lookouts to put up their hands, the lily banner was hauled down and the white ensign run up in its place. The British gave them an offer they couldn't refuse: either guide the ships through the channel or be hung from a mast. The pilots agreed and were distributed among the ships.

Many captains, however, decided to go through on their own. When they saw the channel, they wondered why the French had been so frightened for so long. It was easy, compared to English waters. The captain of the *Goodwill* transport was known as "Old Killick." He had a French pilot, but the fellow irritated him with boasts about how Canada would be the grave of the British and how redcoats' scalps would decorate the walls of Quebec, unless they first drowned along the way.

"Ay, ay, my dear," growled Old Killick. "But damn me, I'll convince you that an Englishman shall go where a Frenchman dare not show his nose."

Old Killick leaned over the bow and began calling instructions to the helmsman. He knew where danger lurked, by the ripple and color of the water; at a glance, his keen eye could tell ledges of rock from banks of sand, mud, or gravel. When the *Goodwill* was through, he stood up, squared his shoulders, and cried for everyone to hear: "Damn me if there are not a thousand places in the Thames fifty times more hazardous than this. I am ashamed that Englishmen should make such a rout about it." The French pilot could only nod and raise his eyes to heaven. *"Mon Dieu!"* "My God, these English are sailors!"

On June 26, the fleet anchored off the Island of Orleans three miles below Quebec. Landing parties quickly overran the island and secured it as a base. Next morning, Wolfe stood at its western tip and looked out across the water. His heart sank. In London, he'd studied whatever he could find about Quebec. Capturing it, he knew, would be difficult. But now he realized just *how* difficult.

Quebec was a natural fortress. The Lower Town, with its homes, warehouses, and docks, lay along the riverside. The Upper Town was perched atop the bluffs. Here was the governor's palace, cathedral, hospital, and citadel. Steep, narrow streets connected both sections of the city.

Steep cliffs two hundred feet high stretched unbroken for miles on either side of the city. No paths led from the riverbank to the Plains of Abraham at the top. Here and there, a few men could climb the cliffs by holding onto rocks and bushes. But a few determined men at the top could hold off an army.

Rivers enclosed Quebec to the west and east. The Cap

Rouge flowed between cliffs and high, wooded banks until it joined the St. Lawrence west of the city. To the east, Quebec was protected by the St. Charles, its mouth blocked by a boom of logs bound with chains and anchored in place. Beyond, the cliffs overlooked a stretch of land known as the Beauport shore. Beauport stretched for six miles, ending at the Montmorency, a swift river that ran through a steep gorge and tumbled over an eighty-foot falls where it joined the St. Lawrence.

What nature had made strong, Montcalm strengthened further. Manpower was no problem; he had fourteen thousand men —regulars, Canadians, Indians—and plenty of artillery to defend Quebec. He set everyone to work digging trenches along the

Quebec as seen from Point Lévis on the southern shore of the St. Lawrence. The drawing, by Captain Harvey Smith, one of Wolfe's officers, is in the British Museum.

cliffs from the St. Charles to the Montmorency. Cannon were placed at key points here and in the city to control the passage upriver. Bougainville was stationed with a thousand men near Cap Rouge to deal with any English who managed to slip past the batteries and come ashore.

Montcalm didn't have to fight in order to win. Victory meant simply holding on, avoiding an all-or-nothing battle until the first frost drove the invaders away; to remain beyond October would mean trapping the fleet when the St. Lawrence froze over. Wolfe's task was the exact opposite. He had about three months to force Montcalm to fight. He could do this either by tricking him down from his trenches or by scaling the cliffs with his redcoats. The young general had plenty to think about when he returned to his tent for his first night across the water from Quebec.

The camp was bedding down for the night when sentries noticed gray shapes gliding downstream. They moved slowly with the ebb tide, heading toward the fleet anchored between the Island of Orleans and Point Lévi, an elbow of land jutting out from the river's southern shore. Moments later, they began to sputter and flare.

"Fire ships!" cried the sentries as they ran for cover.

The French had prepared a warm welcome for their enemies. Nothing is deadlier to sailing vessels than fire. The stoutest ship of the line was merely a firetrap of wood and canvas, rope and tar and gunpowder. Some of the greatest naval disasters have been due, not to storms or enemy action, but to an overturned candle or cooking coals gone astray.

The French had secretly turned seven vessels into fire ships, giant floating torches. Freshly cut pine boughs filled their cargo holds. Decks and rigging glistened with fresh tar. Gunpowder barrels lay on deck, alongside old cannon stuffed with powder and shot. At ten o'clock in the evening, June 28, volunteers sailed their fire ships out of Quebec harbor. Their orders were to come as close as possible to the British fleet, light the fuses, and escape in longboats towed at the stern.

It was magnificent, and terrifying, as if seven volcanoes were erupting at once. Tongues of flame shot from every porthole. Earsplitting explosions mingled with the crackle and hiss of cascading sparks. The sky was crisscrossed with trails of hot iron and burning wood.

The redcoats, landlubbers that they were, cowered at the sight. Not the jackies, the British sailors. Calmly, without rush or fuss, they cast off in longboats. Ignoring the danger, they attached chains to the fire ships and towed them into the shallows, where they burned harmlessly till dawn. These fellows seemed to enjoy danger. "Hello, Jack," a grinning sailor shouted to a mate. "Did ye ever take hell in tow?" Wolfe, however, didn't see the joke. He sent word to Quebec that next time fire ships were used, he would tow them alongside transports with French prisoners aboard. That threat ended the problem.

During the following days, Wolfe set up his main camp on the Montmorency, across from Montcalm's trenches. A large force also landed at Point Lévi, taking it after a short, sharp fight with its defenders. Brigadier General Robert Monkton, his second-in-command, set up his own camp there and moved the artillery into position. Now, with Quebec only a half mile away, the English began to fight fire with fire.

The guns bellowed. Each day, all day and far into the night, tons of iron and explosive rained down on Quebec. A pall of dust and smoke hung over the Lower Town; things became so bad that firemen let clusters of buildings burn without trying to save them. Gunners soon found the Upper Town's range as well. One night, hot shot set some wooded buildings on fire. High winds carried the embers to the cathedral, which burned to the ground in an hour. The hospital went up in flames a few days later, together with scores of patients trapped in the blaze. It was like Louisbourg, only on a larger scale.

Unlike Louisbourg, however, the Quebecers were able to carry the fight almost into the enemy's camp. Frenchmen and Indians, mostly Abnaki, haunted the woods around Monkton's batteries. Sentries were knifed and scalped. Patrols were ambushed and mutilated bodies left to strike terror into their comrades.

This time, guerrilla tactics backfired. Gone were the days when redcoats panicked at the thought of Indians or of Canadians naked and painted as Indians. The rangers had taught them the tricks of forest fighting, tricks they soon tried with success. Redcoats turned their coats inside out and daubed the linings with mud. They stuck leaves into their caps, dulled their gunbarrels with grease, and took to the woods in small groups. Before long, Indians were complaining that redcoats no longer stood still and allowed themselves to be killed.

Wolfe took a hard line against guerrillas. He gave orders allowing his men to scalp Indians and whites disguised as Indians wherever they were found. Moreover, villages on the southern side of the river were to be burned if anyone fired on the troops or sent supplies to Quebec. Yet Wolfe, unlike the enemy, would never make war on helpless civilians. "Women and children," he added, "are to be treated with humanity; if any violence is offered to a woman, the offender shall be punished with death."

Redcoats followed their orders to the letter. Indians were killed on sight and scalped. No mercy was shown to whites dressed as Indians, even though they claimed it was only a joke. The men and boys of the village of St. Joachim were slaughtered when they foolishly masqueraded as Indians.

Montcalm watched all of this from his headquarters at Beauport, satisfied that things were going his way. The Frenchman had plenty of time. He was willing to see Wolfe tear Quebec apart and burn villages along the river, for every day Wolfe failed to bring him to battle was a day closer to winter and victory.

Wolfe knew this and decided upon a desperate gamble. He had noticed that the French had gun batteries at several points along the shore above the highwater line. At low tide, mud flats as much as a half mile wide were exposed from the Beauport shore to the mouth of the Montmorency, where the water was waist-deep for a few hours each day. His plan was to have troops rowed across from the Island of Orleans and landed on the mud flats. The first wave would be grenadiers, elite units trained to throw grenades—metal balls filled with gunpowder and exploded by a fuse lit by a smoldering rope. At the same time, other troops would wade across the Montmorency from the main camp. Montcalm, he hoped, would come down from his trenches to save the batteries, which would allow Wolfe to draw him into a battle. Altogether, seven thousand redcoats would take part in the operation. Wolfe had no doubt that they could whip twice their number of Frenchmen.

On the last day of July, redcoats filed into their assault boats and rowed to the jump-off position opposite Beauport. For six hours, with cannonballs screaming overhead, they waited for low tide. Waiting was harder than fighting. They jammed the narrow benches, sweating in the heat and humidity. The constant bobbing of the boats made men seasick and they leaned over the side to vomit; going to the toilet was a more serious problem. As the hours passed, they became short-tempered and impatient for action.

At last Wolfe gave the attack signal. Oars flashed and the first wave of 800 grenadiers sped toward the shore. Unfortunately, submerged rocks prevented the boats' reaching the assigned landing place. The grenadiers had to leap overboard and, with muskets and powder horns held overhead, wade ashore under enemy fire. Men shuddered and pitched forward amid widening patches of red. Others, struck by cannonballs, were torn apart.

A kind of contagious madness gripped the men who made it ashore. Suddenly, without speaking or waiting for orders, they attacked a French battery with bayonets. Those artillerymen who didn't take to their heels in time were skewered where they stood.

For a moment the grenadiers paused, breathless, while the second wave landed and began to form ranks. Then, as if from nowhere, a drummer boy began to beat the *rap-tap-tap* of the charge, followed by a band blaring "The Grenadiers' March."

That did it. The grenadiers, shouting at the tops of their voices, swarmed past their astonished officers and began to claw their way up the face of the cliff. The French watched in disbelief for a moment, then sent volley after volley of musket balls down the slope, into the climbers' faces. Grenadiers by the dozen rolled down the cliff until caught on a bush or rock ledge, or they bounced onto the beach like rag dolls.

All the while, the black clouds of a summer storm were gathering overhead. Thunder drowned out the noise of mus-

*Montmorency Falls as seen from Wolfe's camp. Here British ships
bombarded the French defenses at low tide, preparatory to landing troops.*

ketry. Big drops began to patter, followed by a blinding downpour that ruined everyone's gunpowder. The cliff side became a cataract of rushing mud. Soldiers, losing their grip, slithered down amid loose stones and wet earth. The French cheered.

Wolfe was furious. His mouth twitched in speechless anger. His bony fists opened and closed as he watched the scene. By taking matters into their own hands, the grenadiers had ruined his plan. Montcalm had no reason to leave his trenches now. There was nothing left to do but order the troops back to the boats and cancel the move across the Montmorency.

As buglers sounded the retreat, Indians, their knives clasped between their teeth, climbed down the cliff to scalp the dead and wounded. When the British took count that evening, 443 men were reported killed, wounded, and missing. It was a disaster.

French confidence soared after Beauport. Quebec might be battered to rubble, but cities can always be rebuilt. What mattered most was the enemy's defeat, and now that seemed certain. "Everybody," recalled a French officer, "thought that the campaign was as good as ended, gloriously for us."

Yet the struggle was just beginning. For within a week of Wolfe's defeat, word came that the English were on the rampage along Canada's southern approaches.

WHILE WOLFE was bombarding Quebec, Jeffrey Amherst set two armies in motion in New York. The first army was made up of three thousand regulars under Brigadier General John Prideaux and a mixed band of a thousand warriors from the Five Nations under Sir William Johnson. In May 1759, this army reoccupied Oswego and began to build a new—larger—fort on the site. Its work done, a small garrison was left behind, while the main force set out by boat on Lake Ontario. Destination: Fort

Niagara, connecting link between Lake Ontario, Lake Erie, and France's remaining forts in the Ohio country.

Outnumbered and outgunned, the French garrison of Fort Niagara was no match for the invaders. The English suffered only one setback when General Prideaux absentmindedly stepped in front of a mortar at the wrong moment; the shell struck him squarely, leaving little to bury. Sir William Johnson took command and finished the siege on July 25. But before the French surrendered, they insisted upon a solemn promise to protect them from his braves. They remembered Fort William Henry and didn't want to be on the wrong side of an Indian massacre.

With the fall of Fort Niagara, all French outposts to the south—Forts Presque Isle, Le Boeuf, Venango—became useless and had to be evacuated. After five years of disappointment and bloodshed, only the British flag flew over the lands watered by the Beautiful River.

On the day after Fort Niagara's surrender, Amherst, to the east, stood with his second army at the neck of the Ticonderoga peninsula. His force, evenly divided between regulars and militia, numbered eight thousand and had masses of artillery. As usual, the general had planned everything carefully and moved slowly, leaving nothing to chance. Weeks had been spent in drilling the troops and disciplining them as they'd never been disciplined before. Gambling was made a whipping offense, along with cursing and drunkenness; several thieves were shot as an example to others. Many of Amherst's men had been with Aunt Abby, and he wanted to rebuild their discipline before returning to the scene of their defeat.

Fort Carillon was commanded by Colonel François Charles de Bourlamaque, an able officer with wide experience in Europe. Although Bourlamaque had thirty-two hundred soldiers, the same number Montcalm had when he defeated Aunt Abby, the situation was different. Amherst, he knew, would make the most of his superiority in artillery. He would blow away the zigzag barricade as if it were built of matchsticks and then go to work on the fort. It would be suicide to resist. The night before the British arrived, Bourlamaque escaped to Crown Point by boat with most of his men, leaving a rear guard to hold out as long as possible.

Amherst's guns were limbering up when a French deserter was brought in. He had good news and bad news. The good news was that the rear guard had slipped away; the fort was empty. The bad news was that they'd left behind a lighted fuse connected to the gunpowder magazine. Fort Carillon was a bomb ready to explode at any moment. Amherst offered one hundred guineas, a fortune to a poor man, to anyone who'd go in and cut the fuse. There were no takers. Toward midnight, June 26, an explosion rocked the fort, turning it into a smoking ruin.

Five days later, as Wolfe's grenadiers were scaling the Beauport cliffs near Quebec, Amherst closed in on Crown Point, only to find that Fort St. Frédéric had also been destroyed. Instead of following the retreating French, he began rebuilding the forts and preparing for a drive on Montreal next year. Amherst's forts, renamed Ticonderoga and Crown Point, may be visited today; each has a museum that explains how it is built and tells its history. During the American Revolution, Ethan Allen and his Green Mountain Boys captured Fort Ticonderoga without firing a shot, "In the name of the Great Jehovah and the Continental Congress." The fort was occupied by the patriots and its guns sent to General George Washington during the siege of Boston.

AMHERST'S NEWS cheered Wolfe but didn't solve his problem. The Beauport defeat hurt him deeply. As commander, he could make no excuses. Just as the full credit for success would be his to enjoy, so must he swallow the bitterness of failure.

Sickly to begin with, weeks of worry, nervous strain, and sleeplessness finally sent him to bed with a high fever. Word raced through camp that the general was dying. This time an army rumor was true. Wolfe himself realized that his time was short. "I know you cannot cure me," he told his doctor, "but patch me up so that I may be able to do my duty for the next few days and I shall be content."

The one thing Wolfe had in his favor wasn't the doctor's medicines—which were useless, if not actually dangerous—but his own willpower. For a while at least, the will to win was stronger than his illness. His mind forced his body to obey. After ten days in bed, on August 29 he rose, dressed, and inspected the camp. The soldiers were shocked when they saw him. His face was drawn, his skin mottled with dark patches. Yet, when they looked into his eyes, those hard, blue, shining eyes, they knew that Jaimie Wolfe still commanded.

Wolfe asked his senior officers—Brigadier Generals Robert Monkton, George Townshend, James Murray, and Admiral Charles Saunders—to suggest how Quebec might be taken. After discussions among themselves, they recommended a landing above Cape Rouge, about twenty-five miles west of the city. The area was thinly defended and offered the best chance of climbing the cliffs in safety. Once on top, they would cut the French supply line to Quebec. Montcalm must then fight to reopen the roads or starve in his fortifications.

Wolfe accepted their plan and immediately put it into operation. He evacuated the camp on the Montmorency and concentrated his army at Point Lévi. Each night, Admiral Saunders slipped a few ships upriver, past Quebec's batteries, until he had a squadron of twenty vessels west of the city.

Now began a game of cat and mouse. Each day the squadron drifted downstream with the ebb tide, as if probing for a place to land. Each night it rode upstream on the flood tide. Bougainville's detachment, which had been increased to three thousand, followed along the cliffs, never losing sight of the ships except on moonless nights, when they moved without lanterns. The idea was to tire the Frenchmen and get them used to seeing British ships that never attacked. When the French became overconfident, *that's* when the blow would fall.

Wolfe, meantime, had made an important discovery. Somehow he found an inlet two miles west of Quebec with an overgrown path winding up the cliff face. The top was guarded by a company of Canadian militia under Captain Duchambon de Vergor, a man despised for cowardice. As if that weren't enough, Vergor had allowed most of his men to return to their farms on condition that they did a few hours' unpaid work on his own land. Here, then, at a place known ever since as Wolfe's Cove, was the soft spot in Quebec's armor.

Wolfe kept the decision to land at the cove to himself, for fear that prisoners might leak it to the enemy. He consulted no one, asked no one's advice or opinion. Officers were told only what they needed to know in order to do their jobs, nothing more. Each worked on a small part of the plan, but the general alone knew how the parts fit together, especially the time and place of the landing. Only at the last moment did he take them into his confidence.

At 2:00 A.M., Thursday, September 13, 1759, two lanterns, their lights shrouded from the northern shore, were hoisted up the mainmast of HMS *Sutherland*. It was the signal to shove off.

A procession six miles long drifted downstream on the ebb tide. Wolfe sat in the lead boat with Captain William Delaune, commander of "the Forlorn Hope." These twenty-four men, all volunteers, were the pathfinders who'd lead the way up the cliff and silence the French sentries at the top.

The general's longboat was followed by scores of others carrying light infantry and Highlanders, the first wave who would secure the beachhead. Behind them came the transports with the second wave, artillery, and supplies. Other troops waited in the darkness at Point Lévi; once the first wave landed, its boats would take them across. Altogether, Wolfe had forty-eight hundred men for this operation.

The advance boats moved swiftly, silently, with padded oarlocks. There was no moon and only the stars gave a faint light. It was like passing through a darkened tunnel, except for the gray shadows of the cliffs looming to the left. The troops sat wedged together, not speaking, thinking their private thoughts.

Suddenly, a quarter mile from their destination, a sentry's challenge rang out.

"*Qui vive?*" he cried, demanding the password. "Who lives?"

Men sucked in their breath; fingers reached for triggers. They could see the white of the sentry's coat against the gray of the cliffs.

At that moment, Simon Fraser, an officer of the Seventy-eighth Highlanders, piped up in perfect French: "*France! Et vive le roi!*" "France! And long live the king!"

"But why don't you speak out?" the sentry cried.

"Hush!" Fraser snapped back. "The British will hear you if you make a noise!"

"Pass, friend!"

The boats continued on their way. Just ahead lay Wolfe's Cove. They grounded with a low, scraping noise. As "the Forlorn Hope" splashed ashore, the sound of distant cannonading echoed off the cliff. Frigates stood on station from Quebec to Beauport, blazing away with every gun. Wolfe had thought of everything: Naval gunfire was to mask the sounds of his landing and keep the enemy's attention focused to the east.

"The Forlorn Hope" scrambled up the path. It was steep, but clumps of brush and roots offered good handholds. Pebbles dislodged by the lead climbers rattled down on their comrades in the rear. Soldiers cursed silently, convinced that the sentries must have heard them by now.

To the Plains of Abraham. In this painting, the St. Lawrence shore is alive with Redcoats. As some climb the cliffs and others are put ashore from the transports, others are being ferried from across the river.

Wolfe, below, strained his eyes but saw nothing. Then the tension broke. From above came the clatter of musketry, followed by cheers.

Panting, their hands and knees scraped raw, Delaune's men crept over the edge of the cliff and crawled forward. They took the French completely by surprise. Captain Vergor fell screaming, a bullet through his ankle, as he fled in his nightshirt. His

men raised their hands in surrender, although a few hid in the brush and escaped.

The cheers of "the Forlorn Hope" were the signal for the light infantry to start up the cliff. Wolfe joined them. A frenzy akin to madness took hold of him. He made his wasted body, exhausted and racked with pain, obey the commands of his mind.

At last he reached the top. It was 5:00 A.M. and sun rays were streaking the sky behind Quebec. Leaning over the cliff edge, he saw the path and the shore below covered with red uniforms. Already boats were bringing the second wave and the troops from Point Lévi.

Wolfe stood up, brushed the dust from his coat, and motioned with his cane. As quickly as his regiments gained the top, they were marched off to their assigned positions. Before them stretched a broad, flat strip of land leading to the walls of Quebec: the Plains of Abraham.

Montcalm was making his morning rounds when a messenger brought a note from Governor Vaudreuil. The general had heard the British cannonading hours before, but had gone to bed when no attack came at Beauport. Now he learned the truth. Patrols had sighted the enemy on the Plains of Abraham.

Montcalm rode closer and, just before 7:00 A.M., saw an awful sight. In the distance, long, double red lines of infantry stretched across the plains. A fine rain was falling, but they stood motionless, as if waiting to be reviewed by their general. A breeze brought the skirl of bagpipes, sounding like a funeral dirge. Perhaps then he recalled the family saying: "War is the grave of the Montcalms."

He knew what those unmoving red lines meant. "Monsieur Wolfe" was daring him to come out and fight. *"C'est sérieux,"* said Montcalm. "This is serious." He had come to the end of the road; there was no way of avoiding battle.

The British stood on the Plains of Abraham, waiting. The rain stopped and the sun appeared. The air was cool, bracing. Wolfe took his place to the right of the British line, in front of the grenadiers. He had forgiven them for their recklessness at Beauport and was honoring them with his presence. They, for their part, were determined to do their best for him today. Snipers were already firing from behind bushes, but there weren't many of them and the redcoats stood their ground without replying.

At 9:30 A.M., Wolfe walked along the ranks, stopping to chat with the troops, giving final instructions, and generally making himself visible. Snipers could easily identify the tall figure in red and began sending bullets his way. Bullets snapped overhead. Bullets kicked up little geysers of dust at his feet. Bullets pinged against stones. He ignored them. Not once did he flinch, or duck, or show fear. He, Wolfe, was the general; his courage had to be an example for everyone.

A captain standing next to him dropped to the ground with a bullet in the chest. Wolfe went down on his knees and, cradling him in his arms, began to stroke his head gently. He thanked him for his loyalty and promised him a promotion when he recovered. The redcoats stood ramrod-straight, but all eyes were glued to their general on his knees. Some had tears in their eyes.

Wolfe himself was wounded moments later. A bullet struck his wrist, shattering bones and cutting muscles. An aide bound the wound with a handkerchief, and Wolfe continued as if nothing had happened.

By now, the French regulars were taking their positions across the plains in the shadow of Quebec's walls. Montcalm rode a magnificent black charger and wore a uniform of green and gold. As he rode along the ranks, he called to the troops. He knew they were tired after standing in trenches most of the night. He encouraged them not with fine speeches, but by appealing to their pride as men. "Are you tired?" he cried, jokingly. Cheers and laughter rose from the ranks. *"Etes-vous préparés, mes enfants?"* "Are you ready, my children?" Again a roar of approval. Then, raising his sword, he gave the signal to advance. A soldier later recalled that he had seemed sad.

Wolfe was anything but sad. A soldier wrote afterward: "I shall never forget his look. He was surveying the enemy with a countenance radiant and joyful beyond description." And no wonder, for he'd reached the high point of his life. Everything he had ever done, he knew, had been in preparation for this day. For the first time in many months, Jaimie Wolfe was happy.

He had started back down the line when a shell fragment tore into his belly. The searing pain would have made an ordinary man double over screaming. Not Wolfe; he was no ordinary man, but a general responsible for the lives of others. If the troops saw him go down, their morale might crack; they might lose faith in themselves. That would be worse than death, for Wolfe. He staggered for a moment, as if he'd taken a false step. Then, squaring his shoulders, he returned to his place with the grenadiers. He arrived just as the French began to charge.

Montcalm's regulars advanced in ranks six deep, a human tidal wave, with Canadians and Indians on their flanks. At a hundred yards, they opened fire. It wasn't a massed fire, but a ragged one, as men paused to reload or reloaded on the run.

The British stood solid as a wall, a long, living wall of red. They stood with weapons shouldered, bayonets shining silver in the sunlight. Nothing stirred, except the regimental flags flapping in the gentle breeze. No one spoke.

Now and then someone shuddered and fell on his face. Another stepped forward to take his place. A soldier of the British Forty-seventh Regiment felt sick. His friend, with whom he'd been standing shoulder to shoulder, had taken a bullet in the stomach and lay thrashing on the ground. He didn't dare step out of line to help him. His friend just lay there, thrashing and screaming, until he died.

Seventy-five yards.

The French pace quickened. Firing increased. More redcoats fell.

At Wolfe's command, the first rank dropped to one knee. Both ranks leveled their weapons at the oncoming enemy. Each musket was loaded with "double trouble"—two balls—for the opening volley.

"Steady! Hold your fire! Wait for the command!" cried the sergeants.

The redcoats were sweating and mumbling curses under their breath. "Froggie," their nickname for the frog-eating French, was hurting them, but they couldn't hurt him in return —at least not right away.

Fifty yards. The French were close enough to count the

buttons on their coats. You could hear their drummers setting the pace, feel the rhythm of their tramping boots.

Forty yards.

Wolfe gave the order.

"Fire!"

The perfectly timed volley sounded like a great thunderclap. Instantly, thick smoke drifted over the enemy, hiding him. But you didn't have to see him to know what was happening. Shrieks of pain rose from within the haze. There were panicky screams and the shouts of officers trying to restore order.

The redcoats reloaded and, as Wolfe had taught them, advanced twenty paces—exactly twenty paces and in a straight line. Then, without aiming, for there was nothing to see, they fired into the smoke.

A wind gust lifted the smoke, allowing the redcoats to see the effects of their shooting. Dazed Frenchmen reeled and staggered like drunkards. Bodies and pieces of bodies littered the ground as far as the eye could see. The wounded groaned, moaned, or sat whimpering. Their comrades—those who could —were running for their lives.

Wolfe gave another order.

"Charge!"

The solid mass splintered into thousands of red fragments. Like hunting dogs unleashed, the British troops bolted after the enemy. No time for reloading now. Today's work would be finished with the bayonet.

Not everyone, however, relied upon this eighteen-inch blade. The Highlanders tossed away their muskets and drew their claymores. Yelling like maniacs, they sprang forward with blades held high. Anyone who fell beneath the swinging steel died instantly. The Highlanders left behind a trail of bodies, each with its head lying a yard away, the length of a claymore blade. One swift-footed fellow hacked off two heads with a single blow.

The Highlanders broke whatever remained of enemy resistance. Both sides remembered Fort William Henry. Indians and Canadians were not offered a chance to surrender, but were hacked down on the spot. French officers overtaken in the chase begged for mercy on their knees, hat in hand, explaining that they hadn't been at Lake George in 1757. Sometimes they were believed.

Wolfe was leading the grenadiers when a bullet hit him in the chest, cutting through both lungs. Two soldiers ran to his side, but he was beyond help. Blood streamed from his mouth and he gasped for air. "Hold me up!" he said, weakly. "Don't let my brave lads see me fall!"

They laid him on a grenadier's coat and unbuttoned his shirt. A grenadier private named James Henderson, himself wounded, held the general in his arms. Wolfe opened his eyes and smiled. "My dear," he said, "don't grieve for me. I shall be happy in a few minutes. Take care of yourself, as I see you are wounded. But tell me, oh, tell me, how goes the battle?"

At that moment someone shouted, "See how they run! They run! They give way everywhere!"

"Who run?" asked Wolfe, opening his eyes.

"The French, sir!"

"Now God be praised. I die in peace." And with that, James Wolfe closed his eyes forever.

Montcalm, meanwhile, had been swept along in the helter-skelter of the retreat. He was riding among his men, trying to rally them, when a bullet passed through his body. It was a death wound. So as not to cause further panic, he asked two soldiers to hold him upright in the saddle until they were behind the city walls.

As he rode through the St. Louis Gate, some women saw him and began to cry: "Oh! Look at the marquis! He's killed! He's killed!"

"It is nothing at all, my kind friends," said Montcalm, struggling to keep his seat. "You must not be alarmed." Five minutes

Death of Wolfe on the Plains of Abraham. The dying general is seen here receiving the news of the French defeat.

later, a surgeon told him that he only had a couple of hours to live. "So much the better," he replied. "I will not see the surrender of Quebec." He died early the next morning and was buried in a shell hole in the convent of the Ursuline nuns; Wolfe's body was returned to England for a hero's funeral.

Thus ended the battle on the Plains of Abraham. It had taken Wolfe three months to set the stage, but had lasted less than fifteen minutes. During that time, the British lost fifty-eight killed; French losses are uncertain, but they may have been as high as fifteen hundred. That night Governor Vaudreuil evacuated Quebec, leaving the city and its people to the conqueror.

Although a skirmish by European standards, Wolfe had fought one of the great battles of history. Other battles still waited to be fought, but the outcome was never in doubt after Quebec. In that quarter hour, Wolfe had decided the seventy-year struggle for North America.

THE WINTER of 1759–1760 was harsh for English and French alike. The redcoats nearly froze in occupied Quebec. Things became so bad that hundreds of British bodies, victims of cold and disease, had to be stored in snowdrifts until the ground became soft enough to bury them in the spring.

Montreal in 1760, as seen from across the St. Lawrence River. The city takes its name from Mount Royal, the great rock dome in the background.

That winter "the White Devil," Robert Rogers, gave the Indians lessons in brutality and revenge. He led his rangers through the snow to St. Francis, an Abnaki village on the St. Lawrence northeast of Montreal. Rangers slaughtered Abnaki, just as Abnaki had slaughtered colonists. Rangers burned their village, just as they had burned New York and New England villages. Then, like shadows, the rangers vanished into the woods.

In the spring, an English fleet arrived at Quebec with supplies and news. Already people at home were calling 1759 "the Year of Miracles." British forces had been victorious all over the world. A fleet had seized the islands of Martinique and Guadeloupe in the West Indies. Another fleet under Old Dreadnought Boscawen had defeated the French at the Battle of Lagos Bay, Portugal. Boscawen's friend, Sir Edward Hawke, destroyed an enemy fleet at Quebron Bay near Brest, France. There were also victories in India and on the west coast of Africa.

Jeffrey Amherst began the final offensive in America during the summer of 1760. Three armies were set in motion toward Montreal, Canada's last stronghold. One army moved west along the St. Lawrence from Quebec, another eastward across Lake Ontario and down the St. Lawrence, and still another north from Fort Ticonderoga. On September 8, Governor Vaudreuil and General Lévis surrendered Montreal. New France ceased to exist after 150 years.

The war continued in Europe until the Treaty of Paris was signed in February 1763. Great Britain gained everywhere, but nowhere more than in America. As the price for returning Martinique and Guadeloupe, she gained all lands east of the Mississippi, except New Orleans, which France gave to her ally, Spain, in exchange for territory elsewhere.

With a stroke of the pen, Great Britain gained a vast empire, one larger than even the Romans had controlled at the height of their power. Yet, with empire, came burdens and responsibilities. And questions. Did she have the wisdom to rule in peace that which her armies had taken in war?

Only time would tell.

⇶ VI ⇇

The Dream
of Pontiac

TOWARD EVENING, April 27, 1763, Indian chiefs and warriors sat around a council fire on the bank of the Ecorse River. The Ecorse is a tributary of the Detroit River, connecting link between Lake Erie and the western Great Lakes. Fort Detroit, French-built but now occupied by the English, commanded that vital waterway.

The Indians had been called together by runners bearing belts of black wampum and red hatchets. Some had come from as far as a thousand miles away. Cree and Nipissing from the northland squatted next to Chickesaw from the Mississippi Valley. The encampment was filled with lodges of other warrior peoples: Chippewa, Huron, Potawatomi, Ojibwa, Delaware, Shawnee, Sauk and Fox, Miami, Ottawa. There were even representatives of the Seneca, who had broken the unity of the Five Nations.

The Indians, streaked with paint and decorated with feathers, sat cross-legged, listening attentively to the speakers. One after another they droned on about their peoples' grievances. The hours passed, slowly, until their host rose from his place. Pontiac. He stepped into the yellow circle cast by the fire, and a hush fell over the audience. The only sound was the crackling and sputtering of the fire.

Everyone knew him—or knew of him. Pontiac was supreme war chief of the Ottawa, the most feared of the western lake peoples. He was about fifty years old: tall, muscular, tough. Naked except for a breechcloth and moccasins, he wore colored stones in his pierced earlobes. His skin, shiny with bear grease, was decorated with tattoos and scars arranged in patterns. Tattooed bands circled his arms, neck, chest, stomach, buttocks, legs, and feet. A large tattooed sun, complete with heat rays and a human face, decorated his chest. He knew the taste of human flesh.

Pontiac had become famous in the wars against the English. He had led raiding parties into New York, rallied his braves against Braddock, and helped ravage western Pennsylvania in 1755. The French so valued his skill that Montcalm gave him a general's uniform as a sign of respect.

Pontiac carried himself with the confidence of one used to succeeding in all he attempted. He spoke in a deep, booming voice, and his words were as poetry to the Indian. Tonight his poetry would be touched with fire.

He began with the story of the Delaware Prophet, a wiseman who had visited the Master of Life in a dream-journey. The Master of Life had created the heavens and earth, the trees, lakes, rivers, animals, and men. Although he loved all his creatures, he loved the Indians best. To prove his love, he had given them the best place in the world for a homeland—the forests of North America. There he meant them to hunt and live in happiness through eternity. All he demanded in return was that they honor him and live as he intended.

Pontiac, war chief of the Ottawa, denounces the English and tells the assembled chiefs of many tribes of his plans to destroy them.

But now the Master of Life was sad, said Pontiac, continuing the prophet's story. His children had broken his laws and forsaken the clean life he'd made for them. They'd listened to the English—"these dogs dressed in red"—and become their slaves. Game was becoming scarce, as the spirits of the furbearing animals fled to their secret villages. Disease and immorality ravaged the tribes.

The Indians, to be saved, must give up the new—evil— ways. They must hunt as their grandfathers hunted, with bow and arrow. English goods—guns, knives, beads, blankets, kettles —must go into the fire. Most of all, the Indians must stop drinking the poison firewater.

Pontiac's story reached into his listeners' hearts. When they were ready, he came to his main point. His voice rose, and his words flew like arrows. A French trader who was there recorded them in his diary: "We must exterminate from our land this nation whose only object is our death. We must destroy them without delay. There is nothing to prevent us. . . . Why should we not attack them? What do we fear? The time has arrived. . . . Let us strike. Strike! There is no longer any time to lose."

Braves sat still, entranced, tears rolling down their cheeks. For deep down, they felt that Pontiac was right. France had been defeated, and now each day brought fresh proof that the victors meant them no good. Unless they acted soon, the Indian way of life would disappear—and with it the Indians themselves.

When the war ended, Major Rogers and his rangers were sent to take over French outposts on the western Great Lakes. Rogers treated the Indians well; he'd seen enough of war and didn't want another if it could be avoided. Unfortunately, those who followed him were more reckless.

During the war, when the English needed Indian help or wanted to keep that help from the enemy, they courted the tribes with gifts and promises of friendship. Yet these were only words, for most Englishmen couldn't imagine that Indians were human beings like themselves. Indians, to them, had no more rights than the beasts of the forest. Officials made treaties with the tribes, but English actions showed their true intentions.

Soon settlers swarmed over the Alleghenies, eager to take the lands that the redcoats had "won" from the French. The French had been good neighbors, content to build a fort and trade; they never claimed the land as their own. English settlers, however, took the land, cut down the forest, and drove away the game. English traders cheated the tribes, exchanging furs for high-priced, poorly made goods. Rum flowed freely, and Indian killed Indian in drunken frenzy. Land speculators, including George Washington, couldn't wait to take over Indian hunting grounds in the Ohio Valley.

Indians knew little of Jeffrey Amherst, and he knew less of them; nor did he care to learn. The commander in chief of British forces in North America sat impatiently in his New York headquarters. Ever since the fall of Montreal, he had been impatient to go home. He disliked America and Americans, and he let them know it with insults.

Amherst disliked Indians most of all. With France defeated, he saw no need for generosity toward "savages" and "brutes," as he called them. As a result, he ordered commanders in the West to take a hard line with the tribes. Indians were never to be given more than a few ounces of gunpowder and a few bullets at a time. All trading was to be done at the forts, not in Indian villages, although tribesmen had to carry bulky furs long distances. Indians were not to be welcomed at the forts. They must enter unarmed, do their business, and get out as quickly as possible.

Amherst's rules startled the tribesmen. They were used to the easygoing generosity of the French, not the stinginess of the English. Worse, they had come to depend upon gifts, especially gunpowder and bullets. In the old days, they had only to ask and the French gave them whatever they wanted. As a result, many had forgotten the ancient ways and were unable to hunt without firearms. It was becoming harder to feed their families, and in some places people went hungry most of the time. Indians feared for the future under English rule.

Pontiac told the council of his own dream. He dreamed of Indian unity, of the tribes burying old hatreds in order to drive the English into the sea. His plan was to attack all the western forts at the same time. Most forts were small, isolated, and poorly protected. The attacks would be sudden, without a declaration of war, so as to take the enemy by surprise. Although France had lost its war, there were still many Frenchmen in the West, especially along the Illinois River. Surely they'd help once the Indian uprising began. When Pontiac finished his speech, everyone agreed to return home to carry out his plan.

What followed was a nightmare come true. In mid-May, all the smaller forts on the Great Lakes and rivers of the West were attacked. Forts Quiatenon, St. Joseph, Edward Augustus, and Miami fell as if by a single blow. Most were simply overrun by superior numbers. Others, like Fort Michilimackinac, were captured by treachery.

Located on the channel that joins Lake Michigan and Lake Huron, Fort Michilimackinac was defended by ninety-five men under Major George Etherington. On June 3, Minivavana, a Chippewa chief, invited the garrison to watch a game of lacrosse between his people and visiting Sauk from Green Bay on Lake Michigan. Lacrosse, as the Indians played it, was an exciting and sometimes deadly game. Often entire villages challenged one another, with the players betting everything they owned on winning. The object was to toss or pass a leather ball over the opponents' goal with a netted racket, or *lacrosse.* The goals were set far apart, and in the charging back and forth the braves could hit one another with their rackets. Broken bones were common, and unlucky players might be trampled if they fell in the midst of a rushing crowd.

The British, bored and eager for a little gambling, accepted Minivavana's invitation. Next morning, Etherington and most of the garrison stood in the shade of the stockade, outside the open gate, to enjoy the game. It was the birthday of England's new ruler, King George III, and a time for celebration.

The braves appeared, stripped to breechcloths and carrying their lacrosse rackets; they were unarmed. Squaws wrapped in blankets mingled with the redcoats near the gate to encourage their men.

The game began. Hundreds of braves dashed about yelling and tumbling over each other as they lunged for the ball. The spectators were cheering, when suddenly, from the midst of the mob, the ball soared toward the open gate. The players swarmed after it.

But as they ran, their yells turned to war whoops. Passing the squaws, they snatched tomahawks the women had hidden under their blankets. The English had no time to run or grab their muskets. Most were struck down and scalped immediately. The fort's parade ground became a killing ground, its buildings the scene of horrors.

Several English traders unlucky enough to be in the fort were chased through the buildings and killed. Alexander Henry of New Jersey saw it all from his hiding place in an attic. He wrote in a book about his experiences:

Through an aperture, which afforded me a view of the area of the fort, I beheld, in shapes the foulest and most terrible, the ferocious triumphs of the barbarian conquerors. The dead were scalped and mangled; the dying were writhing and shrieking under the unsatiated knife and tomahawk; and from the bodies of some, ripped open, their butchers were drinking the blood, scooped up in the hollow of joined hands, and quaffed amid shouts of rage and victory. I was shaken not only with horror, but with fear.

Pontiac wanted the honor of capturing Detroit, largest and strongest of the Great Lakes forts. Detroit was not only a fort, but a trading post of a hundred buildings surrounded by a stockade. Beyond the stockade, along the river, there lived two thousand people—French traders, their families, and assistants. They hated the English but, since the war was over, wanted only to live up to the peace treaty and make money.

Fort Detroit was defended by 125 redcoats, plus 40 English fur traders; several small cannon were mounted in blockhouses and two armed schooners were anchored in the river. Major Henry Gladwin, the commander, had been wounded at Braddock's Defeat. A hard-boiled Scotsman, stubborn and unsmiling, he was more than a match for Pontiac.

Although Pontiac had nearly a thousand warriors from various tribes, he hoped to win cheaply by surprise attack. He sent a message to Gladwin requesting a meeting on the morning of May 7. The major agreed, and throughout the night braves did the war dance around a blazing bonfire.

Pontiac's plan was to enter the fort with sixty of his best warriors. Despite his promise that they'd be unarmed, each would carry a sawed-off musket under his blanket. At a signal from Pontiac, Gladwin and his officers would be shot dead. The rest of his warriors, hidden outside the fort, would rush in at the sound of the shots. Those Englishmen unlucky enough not to be killed outright would be burned in front of slow fires. It was a sound plan, except that a Chippewa girl who loved Gladwin told him everything the night before.

Pontiac knew that something was wrong the moment he set foot in the fort. The guard on the walls had been doubled. Soldiers were drawn up on the parade ground with fixed bayonets. Men stood on the rooftops, armed and ready for anything. Cannon were trained on the gate. It was a trap, and Pontiac knew that a false move would bring a hail of bullets.

The Ottawa faced Gladwin and, looking around, complained about the cold welcome he'd received. "We would be very glad to know the reason for this, for we imagine that some bird has given thee ill news of us, which we advise thee not to believe, my brother, for there are bad birds who want to stir thee up against thy brothers, the Indians, who have always been in perfect friendship with their brothers, the English." Gladwin replied that his dear friend, Pontiac, mustn't be offended by the show of force. He'd ordered his men to arms in preparation for a parade that afternoon. Each man lied, and the other knew it.

The next move was Pontiac's. He took from a beautifully decorated pouch a wampum belt, white on one side, green on the other. Holding the green side toward Gladwin would signal the attack.

All eyes followed his hands. Gladwin nodded and a drum

roll sounded in one of the buildings. Redcoats gripped their muskets and glared at the Indians.

Pontiac held the white side of the wampum toward Gladwin. After some confusion, he led his warriors through the gate, casting evil glances as he went. Once outside, a war whoop burst from his throat. Instantly, bullets pelted the fort like hailstones. Fire arrows flew to their destination. The Indians began a wild manhunt, sparing Canadians but killing every English person caught outside the stockade. Thus began a five-month siege, the longest in American Indian warfare. From May to October 1763, Pontiac kept up the pressure on Detroit. No Indian leader before or since showed such determination in attacking a fort, or in holding the attacking force together.

Like any war chief, Pontiac knew that his people would never stand for high losses. If he was to keep their loyalty, he must fight economically, holding casualties to a minimum. And the best way to do that was to isolate the fort and wait for starvation to do its work. Detroit was cut off from the outside world. War parties roamed the woods, ready to ambush British reinforcements. Canoes full of warriors were hidden along the river to pounce upon relief convoys.

Pontiac began a war of nerves as well as bullets and arrows. At night, warriors beat drums, shook rattles, and shouted threats to keep the garrison awake. One day Pontiac made Gladwin an offer. If Gladwin surrendered, sparing the Indians the losses they'd suffer in an assault, Pontiac would spare the defenders lives. If not, those killed in the battle would be lucky, for all captives would die by torture, beginning with the commander.

To prove that he meant business, a line of Indians, naked and painted black, stepped from the forest. Each howled a death wail and carried a stick with a scalp fluttering at the end. These scalps, Pontiac explained, were all that remained of the garrison of Fort Sandusky on the southern shore of Lake Erie.

Pontiac's Huron allies later trapped a fleet of barges bringing reinforcements from Fort Niagara. They had landed for the night at Point Pelée on Lake Erie when the Huron overran their camp. The survivors were stripped, packed into their barges, and forced by jeering braves to row past the fort. Next morning their burned and mangled bodies floated past the fort from Pontiac's camp. That day Gladwin's cannon fired volleys of red-hot nails. The Indians' cruelties only stiffened the garrison's determination to fight to the death.

Help finally arrived under cover of a fog late in July—barges carrying food, ammunition, and 220 soldiers, including Robert Rogers and 20 rangers. The reinforcements were led by Captain James Dalyell, a brave soldier and a favorite of Amherst's. Dalyell told Gladwin that the general had sent him to end the siege immediately. To do that, he planned to attack Pontiac's main camp at night and destroy it, along with its inhabitants. The camp was only three miles from the fort and could easily be surprised, he believed.

At 2:30 A.M., July 31, 1763, Dalyell led 247 men through Detroit's east gate. The column marched quickly, although noisily; the sound of tramping boots and jangling equipment carried far in the still night air. As usual, Rogers's Rangers followed their own discipline, keeping their distance from the main body. Within an hour, the column began to cross a narrow wooden bridge over Parent's Creek, less than a mile from the Indian camp.

That's where Pontiac caught them.

A Frenchman had slipped out of the fort and told Pontiac of the coming attack. The chief acted without hesitation, sending the Indian women and children into the forest for safety; only old men stayed behind to keep the campfires burning in case British scouts were in the area. The young men were divided into two parties: one to cover the bridge, another to slip around the enemy's rear.

Dalyell walked right into the trap. The moment his column reached the center of the bridge, the Indians opened fire. Spurts of flame stabbed the darkness, sending men tumbling into the water. Their comrades pushed forward, only to be cut down by braves hidden on either side of the path. Dalyell himself fell leading a charge. Had it not been for Rogers's Rangers, who covered their escape, the defeat would have become a massacre. As it was, the English suffered sixty casualties, one-quarter of their force. Parent's Creek ran red with the blood of the men who had fallen off the bridge. It has been known ever since as Bloody Bridge.

The Indians celebrated their victory with a feast. Years later, Colonel James Knaggs repeated a story told by his grandfather, a veteran of Fort Detroit:

After his triumph Pontiac invited the leading French residents to a grand feast in honor of the victory. There was plenty of fish and fowl but no liquors. After the feast was over Pontiac said . . . "How did you like the meat? It was very good young beef, was it not? Come here, I will show you what you have eaten," and Pontiac then opened a sack that was lying on the ground behind him and took out the bloody head of an English soldier. Holding it up by the hair, he said with a grin, "There's the young beef."

Yet despite Dalyell's defeat, Detroit had been reinforced and would continue to be reinforced on foggy nights. Gladwin, stronger than ever, held on with grim determination.

FARTHER TO THE EAST, meanwhile, Delaware, Shawnee, and Seneca moved against the forts guarding the way to the Ohio Valley. These forts—Presque Isle, Le Boeuf, Venango—had been rebuilt after the French war, but were weakly defended. When the Great Lakes forts were overrun, Colonel Henry Bouquet urged Amherst to strengthen these while there was still time. The general refused, and, sure enough, the Indians struck late in

June. One after another, the forts were taken, burned, and their defenders slaughtered. Only Fort Pitt—Pittsburgh—held out, thanks to its large garrison and to its commander, Captain Simeon Ecuyer, like Bouquet a Swiss mercenary in the pay of England.

The fall of the eastern forts opened the frontier settlements to a reign of terror unknown since Braddock's Defeat nine years earlier. Once again, war parties burned their way across Pennsylvania. Once again, wagonloads of bodies rumbled through Philadelphia's cobblestoned streets. Panic spread everywhere, even to New York City.

General Amherst was furious. The Indians, he vowed, would pay dearly for their treachery. Orders went out to field commanders to exterminate "the vermin." Indians must be treated "not as a generous enemy, but as the vilest race of beings that ever infested the earth, and whose riddance from it must be esteemed a meritorious act, for the good of mankind." He didn't want to hear about Indian prisoners; all captives must "immediately be put to death." Commanders must also find ways of giving the warring tribes "gifts" of blankets and clothes from smallpox victims. This horrible disease would, Amherst hoped, exterminate entire tribes.

Frontier people didn't need the general's encouragement to wipe out Indians. A burning hatred swept the frontier. There were settlements in which every family had lost loved ones during raids. They wanted the raids stopped, and they wanted revenge.

The Paxton Boys, a gang of roughnecks from Paxton, Pennsylvania, set out to kill Indians, *any* Indians, innocent or guilty. A few days after Christmas 1763, they attacked the Conestoga, Christian Indians who had lived peacefully alongside whites for generations. Conestoga cabins were put to the torch. Conestoga men, women, and children were killed and their scalps paraded at the end of long sticks.

The Paxton Boys even marched to Philadelphia after those

Conestoga who had gone there for refuge. Benjamin Franklin was shocked, calling them "Christian white savages." Nevertheless, he went out to reason with them. They finally agreed to spare the Conestoga on Franklin's promise to ask the assembly for more money for frontier defense.

The siege of Fort Pitt began late in July 1763. There was never a real chance of its being taken without artillery. Captain Ecuyer knew of Pontiac's uprising and had taken the necessary precautions. In addition to his four hundred men, Ecuyer had heavy cannon, lots of ammunition, and food to last until winter.

. Ecuyer's men were in high spirits and eagerly exchanged shots with the Indians. Whenever a delegation called for a truce to warn of the consequences of not surrendering, Ecuyer scorned their offers of mercy. His soldiers enjoyed seeing him in action. He, not the Indians, held the upper hand, he would shout from atop the stockade. He would advise them to return to their villages to care for their women and children. He didn't want to hurt them, but if they didn't leave his fort alone he would blow them to atoms with exploding shells. Then, stepping back, he would call to his men: "Lie low, shoot straight, and when you see an Indian's head, make sure that you hit it."

They were shooting straight on August 10, when the sound of heavy firing came from the southwest. Ecuyer jumped to the top of the stockade with a small telescope and, scanning the edge of the forest, saw Indians fleeing in all directions. Suddenly redcoats and Highlanders of the Black Watch came into view. Colonel Bouquet had broken the siege and, with it, Pontiac's uprising in the Ohio country. That night the colonel and his friend were seen to smile, a rare sight, indeed; they even gave some of the ladies the pleasure of a dance. Bouquet was especially happy, for only a few days earlier it seemed that he'd lose his scalp.

Bouquet had marched from Carlisle, Pennsylvania, along the road built by General Forbes in 1758. He had brought with him a wagon train and 460 men who knew little of forest fighting. The only advantage was that the Black Watch were disciplined veterans who would follow him anywhere.

On August 5, the column stopped to rest at Bushy Run, a stream about twenty-five miles south of Fort Pitt. It was a place of evil memories, for Braddock's army had been destroyed only a few miles away. The soldiers felt uneasy, as if history was about to repeat itself. It nearly did.

Early that afternoon, snipers began a ragged fire, followed by heavy volleys. The forest swarmed with Delaware and Shawnee, and they meant to destroy Bouquet's force. War whoops seemed to come from every direction at once. Soldiers fell, killed by invisible marksmen. The most anyone saw were figures painted red with green circles under their eyes. No sooner did they see an Indian than he vanished in the underbrush. They understood what Braddock's men had been up against.

But Bouquet was no Braddock. He ordered his troops to break ranks and take cover. Even so, they suffered terribly. After seven hours of fighting, sixty men lay dead or wounded. Worse, they had been forced to the top of a low hill, from which there was no retreat.

Night came, but darkness offered no relief. The hilltop had no water, and the wounded became delirious with thirst. Their comrades had their own problems. Numb from fatigue, their minds racing with thoughts of scalping and torture fires, soldiers lay in a half-sleep. The moment they dozed off, a bloodcurdling war cry would jolt them awake, shaking and with heart pounding.

Bouquet sat with his back to a tree, thinking. To survive, he had to bring his hidden opponents into the open, where his men could deal with them face to face. Reaching back into his memory, into history, he formed a plan. It was a simple plan, based upon a tactic generals had used since Roman times. His troops could fight well and take orders—that he knew. Very well; he'd have them fake a retreat, then attack the enemy's rear.

Daylight came, bringing a fresh hail of lead from the hidden Indians. The fighting continued for hours, the attackers growing bolder all the time. They began to show themselves and to taunt the troops in broken English: "We get you! We get you!" Bouquet watched them carefully, waiting for the right moment. At last it came and he gave the order.

Two companies of the Black Watch had been fighting at the center of the British line. At Bouquet's order they stopped fighting, looked about as if puzzled, and flew to the rear. Seeing this, the Indians were sure that panic was spreading among the enemy. Yelling wildly to increase the panic, they came forward in a mass toward the gap left in the line by the Highlanders.

What they didn't know was that the Highlanders hadn't panicked. Once out of sight, they ran along a hidden trail that brought them to the Indians' rear, where they waited under cover.

They didn't have to wait long. As the Indians charged into the gap, the soldiers on either side turned to the right and left and opened fire. Braves toppled over, but their companions kept coming.

Just then, the Highlanders shouted their own war cry and fired a volley from behind. The Indians turned to meet this new threat, only to see the glint of steel. The Black Watch had tossed aside their muskets and drawn their terrible claymores. Those blades ended the battle in minutes.

IT HAD BEEN a close call. The Indians lost 60 braves, the Scots 115 killed and wounded. But Bouquet had saved Fort Pitt at the Battle of Bushy Run.

News of Bushy Run came as a blow to Pontiac. Fort Detroit had proven itself a tough nut to crack. Each day, Major Gladwin's men fought with growing confidence, while Pontiac's braves grew restless. Ammunition was almost gone, with no chance of getting more. Already braves were slipping away to hunt and build up food reserves for the winter. They sensed failure and were looking out for themselves.

Pontiac, too, knew that time was running out. Toward the end of October, a messenger arrived from the French commander at Fort de Chartres on the Missouri River. His people, he said, were finished with war. The Master of Life had inspired the kings of France and England to make peace, and he intended to live up to its terms. If his Indian brothers were wise, they would also bury the hatchet.

That message ended Pontiac's dream. His authority melted away like an icicle in the sun. Even the Ottawa turned their backs on him. Unable to admit defeat, he packed his belongings and fled westward with his family. Never again would an Indian leader keep white soldiers at bay for so long—not Tecumseh, the Shawnee, or Osceola, the Seminole, or Sitting Bull, the Sioux.

Next spring, 1764, the British reoccupied the burned-out forts and started to rebuild. After receiving heavy reinforcements, Bouquet stabbed into Indian territory with fifteen hundred men. Nothing could stand in his way. By October, his army reached the Muskingum River, within striking distance of the main Delaware and Shawnee villages. He sent them an ultimatum: surrender or die. They surrendered.

Bouquet's peace terms were harsh. There were to be no more white Indians. Every white captive—Englishman, Frenchman, woman, child—must be handed over within twelve days. A woman who'd married an Indian and had half-breed children must leave them behind. People adopted into tribes as youngsters must return to the white world. They weren't *asked* what they wanted, just *told* what had to be done.

On the twelfth day, hundreds of whites were brought to Bouquet's camp. Some came willingly, glad to see their own people once more. For many others, however, the Indians were their people, the forest their home. They answered only to Indian names, spoke only Indian languages, felt comfortable only in Indian clothes. A blanket on the ground next to a fire was the only bed they knew.

It was a time of misery. Indians wept at having to give up those they'd made their flesh and blood. Whites wanted to stay with their Indian families. Children, Bouquet reported, "cried as if they should die when presented to us." Young women "cried and roared when asked to come and begged to stay a little longer."

For a time, many tried to escape. Fourteen-year-old John McCullough, who had lived with Indians most of his life, was returned to his white father. John ran away, was captured by soldiers, and brought back, tied hand and foot. He escaped again and lived with his Indian parents for a year before being retaken and carried to Fort Pitt under armed guard. Women often ran away, risking lonely death in the forest to return to their Indian husbands and children. For them the new life, not the Indian life they'd known, was the real captivity.

Pontiac wandered from place to place for three years, until even he had to admit defeat. In the spring of 1766, he met Sir William Johnson at Oswego to make peace. He buried the hatchet and, having given his promise, never fought again.

But others hated him and wanted him dead. On April 20, 1769, Pontiac visited Cahokia, a village on the Mississippi to do some trading. He was with a Peoria brave named Black Dog who, he thought, was a friend. They had come out of a store and were walking down the street when Black Dog cracked Pontiac's skull with a club and, leaning over his limp form, stabbed him in the heart. Nobody today knows the murderer's motive.

THE FRENCH WAR was over, the Indian rebellion crushed. Great Britain had won an empire upon which the sun never set. Yet, at the moment of victory, she was already in danger of losing her most prized possession, the thirteen colonies. The colonists had many grievances—about taxation, about trade, about the arrogance of His Majesty's military commanders. But as long as they feared the French and their Indian allies, they swallowed their grievances for the sake of the mother country's protection. Now that their enemies were defeated, their grievances were felt more keenly, became more irritating. Even men like George Washington and Benjamin Franklin began to waver in their loyalty.

The French and Indian Wars set the stage for the wider conflict that began in 1776. The subjects of King George III called that conflict the American War. We know it as the American Revolution.

Some More Books

Axtell, James. *The European and the Indian.* New York: Oxford University Press, 1981.

Clark, Ronald W. *Benjamin Franklin.* New York: Random House, 1983.

Colby, Charles W. *The Fighting Governor: A Chronicle of Frontenac.* Toronto: Glasgow, Brook & Co., 1922.

Connell, Brian. *The Savage Years.* New York: Harper & Brothers, 1959.

Cuneo, John R. *Robert Rogers of the Rangers.* New York: Oxford University Press, 1959.

Douville, Raymond, and Jacques Casanova. *Daily Life in Early Canada.* New York: Macmillan, 1967.

Downey, Fairfax. *Louisbourg: Key to a Continent.* Englewood Cliffs, N.J.: Prentice-Hall, 1965.

Eckert, Allan W. *Wilderness Empire.* Boston: Little, Brown, 1969.

Flexner, James Thomas. *George Washington: The Forge of Experience, 1732–1775.* Boston: Little, Brown, 1965.

Hamilton, Edward P. *The French and Indian Wars.* Garden City: Doubleday, 1962.

——. *Ticonderoga: Key to a Continent.* Boston: Little, Brown, 1964.

Heard, J. Norman. *White into Red.* Metuchen, N.J.: 1973.

Hibbert, Christopher. *Wolfe at Quebec.* New York: World Publishing Co., 1959.

Lloyd, Christopher. *The Capture of Quebec.* New York: Macmillan, 1959.

O'Meara, Walter. *Guns at the Forks.* Englewood Cliffs, N.J.: Prentice-Hall, 1965.

Parkman, Francis. *The Conspiracy of Pontiac.* Many editions of this classic have appeared since its publication in 1851.

————. *Montcalm and Wolfe* is a beautifully written book and has been enjoyed by generations of readers since it appeared in 1884.

Peckham, Howard H. *Captured by Indians: True Tales of Pioneer Survivors.* New Brunswick, N.J.: Rutgers University Press, 1954.

————. *The Colonial Wars, 1689–1762.* Chicago: University of Chicago Press, 1964.

————. *Pontiac and the Indian Uprising.* New York: Russell & Russell, 1970.

Roberts, Kenneth L. *Northwest Passage.* Garden City: Doubleday, 1959. A gripping novel about Robert Rogers's raid on St. Francis.

Underhill, Ruth. *Red Man's America.* Chicago: University of Chicago Press, 1953.

Van Every, Dale. *Forth to the Wilderness: The First American Frontier, 1754–1774.* New York: William Morrow, 1961.

Whitton, F. E. *Wolfe and North America.* Port Washington, N.Y.: Kennikat Press, 1971.

Index

PICTURE CREDITS